An Intentional Life

Five Foundations of Authenticity & Purpose

LISA KENTGEN, Ph.D.

© 2018 by Lisa Kentgen
www.drlisakentgen.com

Published in the United States by
Stryder Press
80 Eighth Avenue, Suite 709
New York, NY, 10011

ISBN (paperback) 978-1-7322001-0-4
ISBN (ebook) 978-1-7322001-1-1

Cover and interior design by Jason Anscomb.

Library of Congress Cataloging-in-Publication data is available.

An Intentional Life

Five Foundations
of Authenticity & Purpose

LISA KENTGEN, Ph.D.

stryder press
New York

Praise for

"Lisa Kentgen has written a profoundly practical book. Those who follow the guidance she offers in *An Intentional Life* are highly likely to experience untold benefits."
—Sharon Salzberg, author of *Lovingkindness* and *Real Happiness*

"*An Intentional Life* exemplifies Lisa Kentgen's gift for seamlessly linking theoretical concepts with pragmatic application of change-making practices. She has a way of encouraging fruitful self-examination that is critical for personal transformation. This is a special book, offering pragmatic insight, wisdom, and guidance for the reader's personal journey toward authenticity."
—Lena Verdeli, Ph.D. Director, Global Mental Health Lab, Teachers College, Columbia University

"Lisa Kentgen conveys ideas that are powerful in a knowing, yet soothing and calm voice—free of jargon. Importantly, she provides the reader with ways to make the ideas experience-near, which is essential for real change. Her work comfortably and substantively straddles the mindfulness and Western psychology traditions; written in a conversational tone while thorough and precise in its understanding. This gem of a book will be an invaluable resource for clients to complement the work of psychotherapy. It will be a wonderful accompaniment to readers who have their own mindfulness or meditation practices. It also stands on its own for readers who have never been in therapy or who are unfamiliar with mindfulness practices. I am a fan of this book!"
—Diana Fosha, Ph.D., Director and Founder, The AEDP Institute

Filled with powerful stories and insights, *An Intentional Life* offers an invaluable framework for creating a life of authenticity and purpose. Dr. Kentgen is an expert guide, blending wisdom, warmth, and practical know-how to inspire us to skillfully turn inward and shape a life that intimately aligns with our values. With the world becoming ever more complex – and confusing – we need this book more than ever."
—Rachel Klein, Ph.D., Fascitelli Family Professor of Child and Adolescent Psychiatry, NYU Medical Center

"In this engaging and smart book, Lisa Kentgen takes an approach to a fundamental question—how can we live authentically? —that is both commonsensical and wise. Dr. Kentgen offers clear-eyed, big-hearted guidance for directing and expanding our ability to observe ourselves and our world closely and fruitfully. The rewards of this undertaking—novelty and adventure, balance, and clarity—are within our reach, and Kentgen knows how to help us get there. This is a truly useful book."
—Martha Cooley, author of *The Archivist* and *Guesswork: A Reckoning with Loss*

"Lisa Kentgen's writing and philosophy are as clear-eyed, compassionate, and proactive as the woman herself. This book is a culmination of Dr. Kentgen's distinguished career as a clinician, teacher, and practitioner of mindfulness, providing a roadmap to self-empowerment and authenticity through intentional practices. As a teacher and facilitator, she embodies the qualities put forth in her work. Dr. Kentgen is a force to be reckoned with and this is a book that can change your life."
—Mark Matousek, author of *When You're Falling, Dive* and *Writing to Awaken*

Contents

Part 3: Choosing

Part 4: Acting

Part 5: Allowing

Acknowledgments

Heartfelt thanks to Mark Matousek who offered skilled guidance, valued friendship, and support at the right moments every step of the way. Many thanks to other creative people who worked on the moving pieces that brought the manuscript into book form, including: Deborah Malmud for her developmental suggestions; Mariah Eppes for editorial assistance; Jason Anscomb for a beautiful cover and interior book design; Rebecca Miller and Evan Novis for creative input on related projects. Thanks to Tyler Wagner for helping navigate the social media world. Gratitude to Sarah Deming for input into an earlier draft of the book. Thanks to Bethany Birkett for guidance in my relationship to writing. Thanks to Rachel Klein for teaching me the value of asking helpful questions. Thanks to Diana Fosha for offering me, as a young clinician, powerful tools that help clients access deeper ways of knowing. Gratitude to dear friends who celebrate risk-taking in the name of authenticity. I thank my family for their support and love, my parents, Donna and David Kentgen, and my sisters, Teresa Schader and Michelle Schaefer.

To all of the spiritual teachers, peace and justice activists, and old souls who have been my models and guides for living authentically. There are few direct references in *An Intentional Life*. Yet the written word of wise, contemplative women and men, both living and long dead, has been an essential part of my own path to intention. The influence of numerous dharma teachers is in these pages. I include books written by teachers in the selected bibliography. Retreats with guides like Pema Chodron, Christina Feldman, Stephen Batchelor, Sharon Salzberg, Rodney Smith, Narayan Liebenson, Joseph Goldstein, Tara Brach, and others have helped me access the knowledge that was waiting to come to the fore. Being in the presence of spiritual teachers like the Dalai Lama and Thich Nhat Hanh have inspired me to prioritize an intentional path that extends beyond my personal tribe to include all beings.

Most of all, the co-authors of this book are my clients and students in psychotherapy and other settings. Their courageous, explorative deep dives helped create a language around intention that has deepened my faith in the path I've outlined in *An Intentional Life*. I thank them for enriching my thinking and my life.

Introduction

The Value of Intention as a Foundation for Living

Brian had everything he had ever wanted—a wife and daughter he loved and a rewarding career. Yet, now in his mid-forties, he felt restless and experienced himself as just going through the motions, unable to appreciate the life he had dreamed of achieving. He feared that, despite all he had, he would wake up in twenty years to find that life had passed him by.

Brian was reluctant to look closely at his experience of restlessness and low-level dissatisfaction because he feared that if he looked too closely, he would discover that he didn't want the life he had spent years building. What if, when he discovered the purpose he felt his life was lacking, it wouldn't fit with what he had created with his wife? Could there be room in their relationship for what he sought, or did the lifestyle they shared interfere with a life of greater purpose? He kept this last possibility at a distance because it was intolerable to him.

Many of us who are seeking greater purpose have a similar fear: What if being happy means losing what I have worked so hard to build? If I make the changes necessary to feel more alive and authentic, will I still have the lifestyle I now have? Will my loved ones and I suffer if I make my own happiness a priority? Do I have the courage to prioritize a life of purpose?

Because of fear, we can stay stuck in habitual patterns, trying to discover greater purpose without addressing the deep-seated longing: a healthy longing for a deeper connection to our lives. Unfortunately, this strategy doesn't work because we are not directly addressing how to participate in life in a qualitatively different way.

Brian couldn't resoundingly say "yes" to his life until he looked directly at his experience of restlessness and disengagement with the intent to understand them. Right now, he defined the needed changes in an either/or way. In other words, from a place of fear he understood his alternatives as either staying with this life which contained so much that he valued—and feeling limited within it—or risk losing it in order to feel greater engagement. The latter was not a real option for Brian, so, he currently perceived no viable way out of the dissatisfaction.

Brian's willingness to look closely at his experience of disconnect now gave him the courage to explore the possibility of real change. He realized that he had created a lifestyle without clearly exploring the implications of his choices. Once the results of his choices played out, he then felt beholden to maintain his lifestyle. His lifestyle was so filled with what he thought of as adult responsibilities that now he had no room for himself. There was no room in his schedule or his mind to muse, to dream, and to reflect upon the big, important questions.

Brian was now asking himself deep, and sometimes difficult, questions rather than trying to manage and contain his restlessness. As a result, he accessed internal states he had not experienced in years. These states included novelty, possibility, and the spirit of adventure, as well as angst and even greater restlessness at times. Importantly, Brian felt greater vibrancy—similar to how he felt as a young man, when his ambitions were not yet achieved and he didn't know what life held in store for him. It's not that Brian was viewing life through the eyes of his younger self. But he was challenging the filters through which he had perceived his life up until now.

Brian took risks and made changes in the way he worked, not knowing how these changes would be received. He chose to create a healthier work/life balance in a corporate environment that did not have a precedent for that type of lifestyle, even drawing criticism from a senior colleague in the process. A year into the shift, Brian did not lose standing in the company, though he could not have known this in advance. And occasionally he was less central in making key decisions.

He continued to evaluate and be open to change for the sake of greater ownership of his life. He let go of things he had thought were important, to make room for things that were actually more meaningful. For example,

Brian realized that he had become trapped by maintaining what he now saw as excessive material comforts, things he had before seen as the fruits of hard work and as a manifestation of being a good provider. He practiced ways to live more simply, and came to see this as important modeling for his daughter. He practiced ways to share what was happening internally with his wife. As another example, Brian had previously filled up his weekends with family outings and activities—which left him feeling stressed and irritable by Sunday evenings. Weekends now had unplanned blocks of time and his family occasionally did things without him, which sometimes made him feel like he was missing out. These conscious choices allowed him moments of creative solitude, something he now realized was of central importance. Brian realized that being more emotionally present was of greater value to his family than simply being physically present.

Brian was able to make radical changes by first committing to paying greater attention to what was happening within himself, and in doing so, had access to a much broader range of experience. He realized that even more important than the concrete changes he made (as necessary as they were), was his expanded self-awareness of all that went into his preferences, choices, and actions. Brian was now taking greater ownership of his life. In so doing, he discovered how to behold the life he had, fundamentally transforming his experience of it.

Brian adopted practices that transformed his relationship to himself and, as a result, to his life. These tools are the focus of this book. You will be offered these same tools in the form of Intentional Practices. Whether or not Brian's circumstances resonate for you personally, you will benefit from cultivating similar practices which will enable you to shape your life in increasingly purposeful ways.

What is an Intentional Life?

We live in a world where people are seeking deeper meaning. Paradoxically, our culture's values and habits don't often lend themselves to deep self-engagement. The little ways that we connect are gradually eroding. As we digitally communicate to others around the world, we are simultaneously becoming disconnected from the small moments that matter most, the moments that make us feel like we belong. In the companies where some of us work, narrow definitions of productivity and profits generally fail to explore the importance of quality of life and environmental well-being. Our hyper-productive, short-term, bottom-line, and technology-based culture perpetuates an unnecessary sense of urgency that diminishes the vibrancy of life.

There is another, more rewarding, way of living: with intention. It is only by living with intention that you can experience yourself as authentic and your life as purposeful. When you are authentic, you know yourself deeply and trust your ability to shape your life in ways that align with your heartfelt interests. You have clarity about the conditions as they currently exist, both within and outside yourself, and understand how to best develop and utilize your resources. Living authentically enables you to shape a life of purpose, an ultimately meaningful life in which you experience yourself participating in something greater than yourself.

Intentional Practices are exercises and rituals that foster greater self-understanding, enabling you to deepen and broaden your knowledge of yourself and the world. They are wide-ranging. Examples include: pausing more often, learning to read your body's cues, asking yourself the most relevant questions, and making choices that align with your core values. These practices may be as short as a few seconds or as long as a sustained effort over months. The self-understanding gained from implementing intentional practices will help fulfill one of life's primary tasks, which is to fully inhabit a life that is your own, consciously chosen and not imposed on you from the outside. Bringing intention to all areas of your life, by adopting practices that will be laid out in this book, makes possible the kind of self-examination and agency that leads to personal transformation.

Every one of us has characteristic habits of mind which include ways of perceiving, thinking, evaluating, and acting that run counter to living intentionally. This book provides a framework of how to approach, understand, befriend, and work with your mind. Intimately knowing your mind's habitual ways of responding is the first step in training your mind to help shape the life in which you can be your most authentic and engaged.

An intentional life, first and foremost, is a commitment to training and concentrating attention in ways that enrich your life and the lives of others. What you tend to notice, how you perceive, what you think and believe—none of these are fixed. Your attention is fluid and open to influence. When you understand this, you can consciously influence your attention.

This book examines how we get in our own way, thwarting our best efforts to be authentic. Noticing how you get in your own way is uncomfortable, sometimes painful. You may feel discouraged to discover that your unhelpful habits of mind are tenacious. Don't worry, you are not alone! Compassionately facing how you get in your own way, as it is happening, is key to understanding that you have the power to do things differently. A young woman I work with said it well, "I'm learning that it doesn't help to beat myself up about how I keep getting in my own way. But I also don't want to keep cutting myself a break by not taking it seriously, because that hurts me too."

An increased awareness of when you are doing things in new and beneficial ways is as—or more—important as understanding how you get in your own way. It is important to be aware of all that is right about you. This cannot be overemphasized. We are often more aware of what we do wrong than what we do right. Our brains can more quickly and easily recognize the same old, same old than the new and different. We can be impatient with small gains. Noticing your small steps in the right direction, and then building on them, is fundamental to real and lasting change. And the change that you make is, in fact, a return to your own wise internal guidance system, bringing you closer to your true nature that gets clouded over.

An Intentional Life: Five Foundations of Authenticity and Purpose lays out the five building blocks that will enable you to shape a life of purpose. Placing *awareness, reflecting, choosing, acting,* and *allowing* experience are at the heart of shaping a life of purpose. These foundations are not mutually exclusive and each require skill-building. Unfortunately, we often engage in them automatically and in ways that do not serve our best interests. By developing practices in each of these areas, you will gain clarity on the direction you want your life to move, be able to steer your life in that direction, and enjoy its unfolding.

You will likely never get out of your own way entirely; that's part of being human. Instead, as you learn to modify unhelpful thoughts and behaviors, new ways of engaging in life naturally come to the fore. You then practice noticing and utilizing these new ways of behaving and build upon them. Until, ultimately, you begin to desire placing more attention and effort toward those things that make you feel alive and in concert with yourself, and spend less time putting energy into things that may be compelling but do not contribute to your life's purpose. You now have developed valuable skills at moving toward your dreams that are aligned with what makes you most authentic.

As you live more intentionally, something else also occurs. The external world starts providing opportunities that you never imagined. This is because at every stage of development you can only imagine possibilities within your current knowledge base and world view. Experiencing yourself as authentic, you more readily recognize new opportunities, welcome them, and utilize them. You'll find that, with your new ways of perceiving the world, you already have what you need to shape a life of purpose.

Our personal communities desperately need people to live intentionally. Only when this happens can we, as communities, as nations, and as a planet, shift from an ongoing cycle of reactivity in response to enormous challenges that require evolved engagement to resolve. A small group of thoughtful, intentional human beings can change the world. No amount of scientific knowledge, no temporarily thriving economy, no technological breakthrough can meet our challenges. Yet if more people commit to an intentional life, no challenge is insurmountable.

The Five Building Blocks

The building blocks of an Intentional Life are Awareness, Reflecting, Choosing, Acting and Allowing. You already employ them every day. But you might not make them the object of conscious inquiry or engage them in a way that effectively serves your most authentic self. If you develop specific practices around these core areas, which this book will help you do, your skill at consciously employing them strengthens and deepens, and they become powerful tools for living. The building blocks are not intended to be mutually exclusive categories; they don't occur in isolation. It helps, though, to take each one of them as a separate object of inquiry and practice.

Awareness is intentionally bringing consciousness to something. With increased awareness, you are an alert observer of your thoughts and feelings as they are happening. You are also aware of how you receive the outside world as it comes to you through all of your senses. In contrast, without awareness, these same things, the substance of all that influences you, passes through the gates of your attention willy-nilly and unnoticed. Unnoticed, you are not in a position to do anything about it.

Awareness cannot be separated from the other four foundations and is the mother lode of experiencing yourself as authentic. Bringing increased awareness to everything you do is at the very core of being the central actor in your life. In this section, you will have the opportunity to examine your core values and the importance of aligning them with your choices and actions. You will also explore the difference between what you desire and what makes you happy to help you escape an endless cycle of searching for more. The essential skill of pausing is introduced, an anchoring practice of stillness, which brings you back to what is happening in the present moment. You will be encouraged to observe the subtle fundamental elements of your experience, those of constriction and openness, which enable you to cultivate the conditions that foster a greater sense of vitality and aliveness.

Reflecting, the second building block of intentional living, requires practice in more directly noticing your experience, which allows it to more meaningfully impact you. Practicing the invaluable skill of asking yourself the most relevant, helpful questions, and then sincerely listening to your responses, enables you to cultivate a deeper understanding of how to effectively shape your life. This section focuses on how thought and language both clarify and obfuscate a deeper understanding of your experience and your world, as well as how they both connect and separate you from yourself. Intentional practices on reflection will make your thinking more creative, and help you make better choices and implement effective action. This section explores how to bring skillful reflection to all experience, expanding it rather than limiting it.

Choosing is the third foundation of an intentional life. The rapid-fire assessment of conditions that exert influence over your decisions usually happens outside of awareness. This section aims to help you bring greater conscious awareness to your choices. You are offered tools to help you become a better decision-maker, including how to make room for greater possibility and how to envision concrete steps toward big dreams. The greatest impediment to choosing wisely is fear, and this section helps you work with fear so that it doesn't interfere with making important decisions. Choosing with intention frees you to take meaningful risks without the pain of future regret.

Acting wisely is the fourth foundation of an intentional life and this section explores how to know how and when to act to in order to build the kind of life and world you want to see. Wise effort includes acting as well as restraint from action, non-striving action, and being proactive rather than reactive. To be an effective actor, value effort over outcome, which helps you commit resources while remaining flexible in how you move toward your goals. Intentional practices in acting help you know when to persist and when to move on, and move more easily through natural and inevitable periods of stuck-ness.

Allowing, the fifth foundation of living intentionally, is challenging for many of us because it is counterintuitive to Western habits of mind. The more you allow (by letting go of all the unnecessary overlay that interrupts experience), the more possibility that exists. Because you are hard-wired to do, think, and act, allowing can initially feel passive, but it is actually very active. The skill of allowing, in combination with a ground of intentional practices in the other four foundational areas, leads to the state of abundance. Abundance is the remarkable byproduct of an intentional life, infusing all experience with purpose and deeper meaning.

Each of the book's sections explain central concepts in the foundational areas of awareness, reflecting, choosing, acting and allowing. There are exercises within the chapters for you to try out different intentional practices. At the end of the book, there is a list of intentional practices by chapter that can be used for future reference. Even though each chapter highlights one core area, the practices associated with each chapter at the end of the book will reflect all core areas in order to heighten the learning experience.

Intentional practices are generative: the examples provided in this book are by no means exhaustive. With continued effort, you will create your own flexible repertoire of intentional practices that become woven into the fabric of your life.

I am a psychologist by profession. Throughout the book, along with personal examples, I present client vignettes as a way to bring the ideas in the book to life. In order to protect anonymity, names and details have been changed and clients are presented as a composite.

You can approach the book in different ways. Simply reading the book with focused attention is an intentional practice. To deepen the experience, commit to a month, a week, or even a few days to focus on testing out the concepts and practices in each section. It helps to set aside time, as little as ten minutes, to practice each day. If you carve out time first thing in the morning, it can help you implement intentional practices throughout your day. Try out the practices in different environments—at home, at work, during uncommitted or play time. Notice where and when they are easier, and more challenging, to implement.

Practices are only helpful in the doing of them. It is important that testing out the ideas in the book not be primarily an intellectual exercise. For example, after trying one out, you might ask yourself, "Is this helpful?" If so, "In what ways is this helpful?" And, "What might be a next step for me?" The exercises offered are intended to support your efforts as you develop ways to personalize your path toward greater authenticity and purpose. As in all forms of learning, the more varied the modalities in which you practice, the more diverse your understanding and the more integrated and deep-seated the knowledge you obtain is.

If you find yourself reading while not feeling engaged, try to reengage or consciously put the book down and pick it up later. Take a break and do something that engages you. For example, listen with absorption to music or a podcast, or go to that museum exhibit you are curious about. Read another book, have a conversation with a dear friend about things that really matter, or take a walk somewhere where there are trees. Work at the pace that best suits you, but stay at it. The more personal your approach to intentional practices—made personal by concretely testing out the ideas for yourself—the more you will get out of it. Eventually you will develop your own repertoire of practices that you will have at the ready for anything that arises.

It is my hope that this book will be a helpful companion in clarifying and moving toward your deepest aspirations and shaping your life accordingly. Take from it what is helpful and integrate it with other ways of learning. While becoming increasingly authentic is a deeply personal process, you can't do it by yourself. Of course, practicing intention in the stillness of solitude is invaluable. At the same time, you will more likely continue to practice intention by sharing your efforts with others as a means of support. Finding friends and a community that support this lifestyle is so important. Integrating intentional practices into your daily experience takes time. Stay at it! You will likely see some benefits early. But the lasting benefits often sneak up on you, when you discover you have crossed a threshold into a qualitatively different place. In this new place intentional practices are now central and you are more attune to yourself and the world around you.

Part I

Awareness

Chapter 1

What Matters Most and Core Values

The most important thing is finding out what is the most important thing.
Zen monk Shunryu Suzuki Roshi

What do you care deeply about? What moves you from within and enlivens you? What does the world most need from you? Your answers to these questions speak to what most matters to you. What are the first things that come to mind when you ask yourself what matters most—your relationships, long-term goals and aspirations, your values? To live with intention, be clear about what matters most and make time for it. This might sound obvious, but daily pressures and responsibilities make it difficult to hold what matters in the front of your awareness. Too often we are in a state of waiting until there is more time and resources to commit to priorities. Don't wait. Meaning doesn't find you. You create it by prioritizing what matters.

If you made a pie chart, how much time would be allotted to what you hold most dear? And of the time you spend, what percentage of that is engaged, quality time?

Exercise: A Way to Explore What Matters Most

This three-part exercise is intended to help you connect with what matters to you. It is best done in two or three separate sittings with a short period of time in between. Write your responses as if no one else will be reading them.

1) Take three pieces of paper and fold each in half. In the left column, write one thing that matters most to you. Do this relatively quickly. Don't edit yourself—continue without stopping. Write a paragraph or so for each thing that matters most. Include what it is that makes what you have chosen so important to you. When you can no longer write without pausing, put down the paper and revisit it later.

2) At least an hour (and up to a day) later, return to the first part of the exercise and unfold each of the three pages. Take a couple of minutes to reflect on what you wrote on each page, one at a time. In the right column, next to what matters most, write down ways in which you make time for what is in the left column. Do you give it priority? If so, how? Be as specific as possible. Think of as many ways as possible.

3) For the final part of this exercise, turn each of the three pages over. For each item that you hold most dear, write down one thing that you will do in the coming three weeks to affirm its importance. Each week, follow through with one. It does not have to be a grand gesture, but it needs to be sincere and heartfelt. Carry it out in a way that honors what matters most to you. After you follow through each week, notice what thoughts and feelings arise from having done so.

To prioritize what matters most to you, it helps to think about how these things personally impact you. What is it about your important relationships that you value? How do these relationships impact you and add to your life? For example, you might value your best friend because you can always be yourself around her. Or your child evokes feelings of tenderness and an intimacy you never before experienced. Your career may be what matters most because it challenges you and you feel valued for your talents. You love running because it is the only time you can get away from a constant stream of thoughts and relax. Maybe meditation matters most because it enables you to be more present to your life every day. Or climate change matters most because without a planet everything else that matters is moot.

Disappointment Creates Opportunity

Sometimes it seems that no matter how hard we try, we just can't manifest what we most value. Maybe we can't break into a chosen field or get the job we've trained for and worked so hard to get. Or we are tired of dating and being single. When we are disappointed that things are not what we thought they'd be, or ought to be, there is the opportunity to open up to things as they really are.

There is great freedom in this path. This is a true starting point for growth and transformation. It is an opportunity to evaluate if what we believe matters most is really true. If it is, for goodness sake, continue in our efforts to manifest it. At the same time, it is also an opportunity to evaluate how we are approaching what we most want.

Stefan wanted to be an actor. He studied hard and graduated from a respected acting school. He had been going on auditions for months, with close calls, but nothing had come through to fruition. Stefan was angry and resentful. He believed he had done everything he could and that life was unfair.

Stefan came to work with me when he was feeling depressed and was re-evaluating his life's course. I asked him if being an actor still mattered most to him and he said yes. The next step was to explore what it meant to Stefan to be an actor. It turned out that he loved the work, and when he had the opportunity to act, he just knew that this work could give his life purpose. He believed his inability to stick the landing at auditions was an unfair reflection of his worthiness as an actor and as a person. We all want external validation, but Stefan was giving too much power to it. He was making his self-worth contingent upon it and this was thwarting him.

I encouraged Stefan to take concrete steps to practice his craft in other ways. Could he reconnect with colleagues from acting school, participate in local theatre on the outskirts of New York City, see more theatre, or get cast as an extra? Taking steps when you feel stuck or thwarted creates internal space, which helps you persist and create new opportunities. Stefan was initially resistant to these ideas because they were not how he imagined his career ought to be progressing. Yet he was having difficulty coming up with his own next steps for himself. So he was willing to take a step despite his resistance.

The first thing he did was reconnect with two friends from his acting program. It was emotionally difficult to reach out because he felt like a failure. But as soon as he did, he experienced camaraderie and support. They had stories similar to his own in that they hadn't had success at finding paid work. But they did have ideas and were involved in acting in different venues. Stefan felt less like a failure and was motivated to find acting opportunities that he had not before considered. He felt humbled when he reflected on how he thought of himself as special and different from his fellow actors. Stefan previously thought this belief helped him persist, but now understood that it did not. By spending time with his acting school friends, and being introduced to other actors, he saw how many talented people were also trying to break in as actors. And they were willing to make the most of opportunities to practice their craft and make connections while doing so. Stefan believed in his talent, but he no longer needed to compare himself or feel superior to others.

As Stefan pursued and created opportunities to act, he felt more connected to the reason why he took up acting in the first place. This affirmed, in a very personal way, how acting mattered to him. He was able to value the process of acting as central to his well-being over the result of a particular audition. Stefan now understood how his earlier belief that things ought to be different than they were got in the way of staying open and creating opportunity. The initial disappointment that brought him through the doors for therapy became a chance to dig deeper and understand his motives, and to pursue his dream of acting without the emotional albatross of resentment and feeling that life was unfair.

Core Values Are at the Heart of An Intentional Life

"What are your underlying beliefs about a well-lived life?" "What qualities would you be most proud to model for others?" "At the end of the day, how do you most want to be remembered?" "If money didn't matter, would you hold the same personal values?" How you answer these questions speak to your core values.

Core values are timeless, unlike your goals, which can change over time. Core values reflect how you fundamentally see yourself, or would like to see yourself. Having clarity on your personal core values enables you to experience yourself as authentic. But it's not enough to know what your core values are. To live intentionally, they need to be central to your life's mission.

Core values are influenced by your upbringing and your culture. But as you increasingly listen to your own internal voice, your core values become more personal and unique. You place your own individual stamp on them. If you asked your immediate family to list their personal core values, there would be diversity. And if there was overlap, and each person then defined what the value meant to them, there would be further variation.

Much is spoken about core values in corporate culture. Too often, talk about core values sounds more like a branding exercise. Yet the relatively rare, truly innovative, and visionary companies make core values central to everything they do. It is their fundamental reason for existing other than making money. Making money does not take precedence over the company's core values. They work hard and consistently to align their vision and goals with the company's core values. They hire employees who share these values. Alignment of core values with all aspects of company culture is absolutely central to what makes great companies visionary. We would benefit from more language and dialogue about how to make individual lives visionary.

An important question for living intentionally is: "Are my core values reflected in all I do—in my thoughts, choices, and actions?" For many of us, there is a discrepancy between our idea of our values and our ability to manifest them in our daily lives. More than any external condition we will face, this discrepancy between core values and their embodiment in our lives interferes with the ability to experience life as purposeful.

Become a visionary in your own life. What are your personal core values and how do they align with your raison d'être? Can you clearly identify how you practice your values in your life, particularly in those areas you define as mattering most to you? Where is there conflict between your core values and your goals? When there is misattunement between your values and your day-to-day life, can you bring them back into balance? When you reflect on these questions, and can answer them in the affirmative, you will experience your life as purposeful.

The following is a list of possible core values: accountability, assertiveness, autonomy, balance, belonging, boldness, broad-mindedness, candidness, capable, care, challenge, civility, commitment, community, compassion, competence, connectivity, conscientiousness, consistency, contemplation, cooperation, courage, creativity, credibility, curiosity, decisiveness, dedication, deliberateness, devotion, diversity, empowerment, enthusiasm, entrepreneurship, equality, equanimity, excellence, fairness, faith, fearlessness, focus, forgiveness, freedom, generosity, genuineness, gratitude, industriousness, innovation, health, helpfulness, honesty, humility, humor, inclusiveness, innovation, integrity, intelligence, joyfulness, justice, kindness, loyalty, mindfulness, modesty, nurture, open-mindedness, openness, originality, ownership, passion, patience, peace, persistence, positivity, presence, reliability, respect, responsibility, safety, self-discipline, sensitivity, service, simplicity, sincerity, solidarity, support, sympathy, tenderness, tolerance, tranquility, truth, understanding, uniqueness, warmth, wellness, wisdom.

Which personal core values do you naturally orient toward? They may be ones you strongly identify with or ones you aspire to. They may be qualities you admired in people when you were young. Looking at this list, you might think, "So many of these are my values. How can I know which ones are core?" Ask yourself directly, "If no one judged me, if I was valued for who I was, what qualities would I most want to embody?" If unsure, which ones most resonate for you, which ones naturally speak to you? You have time to test them out, modify, or change them as you develop practices around them.

Defining your core values for yourself is important because without clarity on your personal definition of them, your values can constrain you rather than guide you. For example, say loyalty is a core value of yours. Loyalty to what or to whom? What if loyalty to someone or something is at odds with something else that you deeply value? In this case, understanding the parameters of loyalty, as defined by you, promotes authenticity rather than hinders it.

Don't relate to your core values as an abstract idea. Be specific. It is difficult to have a deeply personal relationship to your values before they are tested in some way. It is by defining values in the particulars of your life that they can be tested out. The more clearly and concretely you embody your core values in everything you do, the better you can mold your choices and actions to be in sync with them.

Align Your Core Values with What Matters Most

The question of what matters often comes up when we experience conflict, or when a crisis happens in life and the rug is pulled out from under us. Crisis and loss are important times to reaffirm core values. At the same time, self-imposed crises can sometimes be avoided if we develop skills to shape our decisions and actions to align with our core values from the get-go.

In the introduction, you met Brian, who came to therapy during a personal crisis in which he felt a lack of deeper purpose. Fueling this crisis was a lack of alignment between one of his core values (creativity) with what mattered most to him (his wife and daughter). His experience of himself as creative played out almost exclusively at work. At home, he cultivated other important values, like safety and love. Brian felt sadness when he recognized that he did not bring his creativity to his home life, the cost of which was a diminished experience of vitality. This recognition was new and important.

Brian incorporated intentional practices to help him infuse the spirit of creativity into his family time. Understanding that this was his central challenge, he could bring his generative problem-solving self to the fore. He relaxed his identity as "dad the provider" and showed more sides of himself to his daughter, feeling freer to be silly and playful at home. Brian now understood that being a provider did not have to fall into the narrow confines of his current lifestyle. Even as he continued to have financial abundance, the focus shifted to more meaningful ways to be present to his loved ones. This shift was an important modeling for his daughter. Brian took pressure off himself—recognizing that he had had high expectations regarding how to be the manager for all of his family's needs—and that this role wasn't fun or enlivening. He could now get helpful distance from assumptions he had unconsciously adopted as his life unfolded, assumptions that had undermined his ability to take the risks necessary to align his choices and actions with his personal core values.

Brian recognized for the first time how vital it was to understand his personal core values and to allow them to shape all of his decisions and actions. Now he was consciously living in greater alignment with his core values in the areas that mattered most to him. This transformation was central to his reclaiming ownership of his life and regaining a sense of purpose.

Exercise: How to Embody Your Values

Look through the list of values on p. 28 or create your own without looking at the list. Write down up to ten that you feel are your personal core values. Then, of these, choose two or three that will become the focus of your awareness. Each value gets its own sheet of paper. Write down a definition for each. Do this without looking at a dictionary.

Under each definition, write down at least one example from your personal experience in relation to how you implemented this core value. If you want to go deeper, below each example of how the core value manifests in your life, also write a time when the core value was challenged in some way.

Finally, for each core value, reflect upon one way you could manifest it in relation to what matters most to you. Return to the earlier exercise on what matters most and imagine one concrete way to infuse your value into what you identified as mattering most. For example, if you said in the first exercise "my career" and a core value is "courage," then what is one way you can bring courage to your career? It is important to focus on real, doable steps, no matter how small. If you want to go even deeper with this exercise, focus on one core value for at least one month. Place your awareness on this core value, reflect upon ways to cultivate it. Then create a clear, simple plan and implement it.

Chapter 2

How to Access What You Need for Well-Being

But what is happiness except the simple harmony
between man and the life he leads?
Albert Camus

If you are reading this book, it is likely that you already have the basic ingredients for well-being: having enough, physically and emotionally; being aware of your basic dignity and worth; living within your means in order to have resources to put toward what matters most; and having supportive and loving relationships. If you have these, you have everything you need.

Well-being is not something that you are lucky to have or unlucky not to have. It is not the result of a set of fortunate external circumstances, though these might exist. Nor is well-being necessarily diminished by hardships though these, too, may exist. It is instead an internal state that is available to you independent of any external circumstance. The sooner you accept that well-being is possible for you, the sooner you can cultivate and access it.

Some people have natural tendencies that enable them to more readily experience well-being. They naturally think more positively, appreciate their bodies and take care of its needs, create time for leisure and play, have creative outlets, perceive abundance and opportunity rather than roadblocks, orchestrate circumstances that feel purposeful, and engage in rewarding personal relationships and work. Other people are more likely to perceive their world, make choices, and act in ways that interfere with their well-being and perpetuate struggle. Most of us, though, have tendencies which promote well-being as well as those which interfere with it.

Although you may have the basic necessities for well-being, you might not experience this as a reality. What is *enough* is a moving target for some people, leading to a constant search for more. Some people link their sense of worth to external validation, which makes the experience of authenticity tenuous at best. Others might love and be loved, but not be able to bring the best of themselves to their relationships. Some people are so hungry for what they do not have that they can't appreciate what is here for them right now. When we are blocking access to states of well-being, this becomes the focus of intentional practices.

Mood is Mixed Up With Well-Being

Moods are often mixed up with the sense of well-being. When this happens, feelings and moods get labeled as good or bad. This leads to problems when certain experiences are avoided because they are associated with negative moods. When this happens, we become cut off from important aspects of our experience.

Positive emotions are an important predictor of well-being. But what is more important than the amount or frequency of positive emotions, is that you take care to place awareness on that which is affirming. If you more naturally notice what is wrong or negative, placing awareness on your tendency to gravitate toward negativity is the first step to opening up to a fuller range of experience.

You can't be your most authentic self unless you open up to all of your experience: positive, negative, and in-between. Negative mood states don't prevent you from experiencing well-being. On the contrary, it is important to allow room for painful emotions whenever they arise. When you push away difficult emotions and experiences, you are inadvertently intensifying your pain because you are compartmentalizing it. When this happens, you limit your capacity to move through the experience and reach the other side of it. It's natural to want to cultivate positive states such as joy, contentment, and excitement. But don't chase these states in lieu of being present to all experience.

In the future, when you look back on your life, you will not think about it in terms of a predominance of mood states. What will endure in your memory won't be the number of positive feelings or pleasurable experiences you have had. Rather, what will likely stay with you are poignant moments: the time you met your best friend or partner, had a creative breakthrough, chose to leave a career to be more fulfilled, moved to a new home, took a life-altering trip, said goodbye to your child leaving for college, revealed yourself in new ways to a friend, gathered up your courage and said "yes" to something or someone in spite of fear, entered a new relationship, or courageously took a risk and redefined an existing relationship. The moments that leave an indelible print are those that occur when you allow yourself to be vulnerable and take risks in the service of living in alignment with your core values.

What is Deep Happiness?

Happiness has been defined in countless ways over centuries. While there are common threads to most modern definitions, research has shown few clear relationships between particular life circumstances and the subjective experience of happiness. This is important because often we strive to change our external circumstances, with the notion that when we do we will be happier. This belief sometimes leads to making decisions and taking action that can actually make us less happy.

Exercise: Cultivating Well-Being

Create a list of things or activities that give you a sense of well-being. Keep this list in plain sight. Include only things that enrich your life rather than things you *should* do because they are good for you. (This is because *shoulds* are often experienced as deprivation.) For example, instead of "smoke less weed" you might instead include other ways that you relax, such as "listen to a relaxation podcast before turning out the lights."

Make the list as specific as possible. So instead of "spending time with friends," use more concrete examples. "Dancing salsa with Olivia," "Having a spa weekend with my closest friends," "Golfing with Charlie," or "Hiking at Harriman State Park for the day with my dog." Or, instead of "getting physically fit" can you list five particular things, such as "that special kind of muscle ache when I pushed myself to the limits at the gym" or "the clarity I feel when cutting down on sugar," or "getting up from sitting every thirty minutes to do ten burpees."

Include on this list a variety of things that take anywhere from two minutes to an entire day. For this exercise, it is especially helpful to include a good amount of possibilities that take no more than five minutes. Activities don't all need to be actions. They can, for example, be setting aside time to reflect upon the good things in your life, or "Telling myself something that is right about me."

Now, every single day, incorporate one of these activities. This is why the short exercises are so important. They make it possible to follow through with this beautiful intentional practice regardless of how busy you are. As powerful as the particular things you do to develop well-being, the consistency of the practice—making it second nature—has mighty benefits.

Deep happiness, as defined here, requires that you know how to cultivate well-being, but it is not synonymous with it. Unlike well-being, which with practice you can come to have much of the time, deep happiness is episodic—experienced in moments. While these moments are not continuous, they become deeply entrenched in your cellular memory. They stay with you and give meaning to your life. The state of deep happiness is akin to a feeling of profound connection—connection to yourself, to others, to everything.

There is converging scientific evidence that bringing the quality of greater presence to all of your activities leads to a greater sense of happiness. One study from Harvard, with over 2,000 college students participating, found that while the students' minds wandered much of the time, being more attune to what was happening in the present moment made them happier. And thinking of the past or the future, even if their thoughts were on pleasant things, made them less content. A major takeaway from the study is that it is natural for our minds to wander, a lot. And, also, wandering minds don't serve our happiness.

Looking to the Whats for Happiness

Even as more and more people understand the importance of being present, and engage with various mindfulness practices, we can continue to have unarticulated deep-seated beliefs that what makes us happy is something external to ourselves. Even though we may know on some level that happiness comes from within, our efforts and energy are often directed toward finding and obtaining things outside ourselves that we believe will make us happy.

Too much emphasis is put on the *what* when seeking happiness: e.g., the content of our work, external recognition of our efforts, our success or the success of our partner, the best school for our children, the composition of our family, our material resources. We look to the *what* to fulfill us. While the *what* is, of course, important, the way we look for it—and at it—is often backwards.

The content of your life—who you love and befriend, your lifestyle, what you do for work—makes you happy only when experienced from within. What matters more than the *whats* of your life is your capacity to savor and be grateful for what is here right now. It is not even the nature of these opportunities, however important they may be, but the fact that you personally perceive them, open to them, help create them, and act upon them.

By focusing on how you approach your *whats* and bringing greater awareness to them, you will naturally gravitate toward the *whats* that are most meaningful to you. This is true in how you choose relationships, how you engage with work, what you do for fun, and how you take care of yourself.

⁓

Roberta, a vivacious woman, exudes confidence and *joie de vivre*. She has a high-powered career and a family she cherishes. For years Roberta has experienced conflict between these two aspects of her life. Both family and work are enlivening to her, yet she has difficulty finding energy for both. In the past year, she carved out time in her overly full life for thirty minutes of meditation on most days. This practice ushered in an awareness of how to make more room for all of it—the messiness of her full life. Since she began meditating, Roberta has ease and well-being that until now had eluded her. She is experiencing more moments of deep happiness that she describes in the following way:

"Even though everything doesn't always go smoothly or as I would like—not by a long shot!—the difference for me now is that I am aware, almost all of the time, of how fortunate I feel to have this life. And, more than before, I experience it as me having it. I told my husband the other night that I could die tomorrow and be happy, and he thought I was being morbid! I'm not planning on dying soon, and I hope I stay around for a long time. Still, there's something about how good where I am feels, that I can't help thinking about death and being OK with it."

Roberta is relatively young, in her mid-40s, and probably not close to death. Her husband's belief that it is morbid to associate deep contentment with death is a common misconception. It is anything but. When we are most present to our life as we are living it, when we are most deeply happy, we are more aware of the finiteness of life, and comfortable with it. This is not morbid at all. It is life-affirming.

A Curriculum for an Intentional Life

If I could implement one thing in the world to change it for the better, it might be to have every school adopt a curriculum in developing the quality of presence. Unfortunately, school curriculums don't typically include guidance in meaningful self-reflection, and in methods to understand what you most value and how to shape life in a way that promotes well-being.

This curriculum would help children develop skills in contemplative practices, in becoming comfortable directing their attention inward. They would learn to notice what enlivens them and to develop their budding core values, and how to put these values into action. They would develop the skills needed to come to trust their unique internal voice. This kind of exploration, much more than a content-driven curriculum, would help kids ask themselves the most relevant questions and provide a method for seeking answers to those questions. A mandatory part of this curriculum would be to build in time to do nothing, a focused *unplugged* nothing, to create internal space free from distraction.

A few years ago, I facilitated a mindfulness group for teenage boys who came from over-crowded, underfunded schools and "at-risk" neighborhoods. The boys were intelligent and had academic promise, but had some catching up to do to help them meet that promise. The umbrella program under which I ran the group provided an environment to help them prepare for entry into good colleges.

One night in the group I asked the boys about their interests—what types of activities excited them, what kinds of environments they worked best in, what their strengths were. They had not considered these types of questions before, or at least had not had conversations around them. I wasn't so interested in the *what* but, rather, the qualities of the *whats* that could help them understand themselves more. The boys had clear ideas about what they liked and did not like, what they liked about themselves and the personal challenges they had, and spoke animatedly.

"I'm good at science!" "Oh, man, I hate science, I'm good at math." "Math is OK but Ms. Smith is a tough teacher." "I like Mr. Roberts, he knows how to keep us awake and he is funny." "I make people laugh, even Ms. Smith can't help but laugh at my jokes." "I like classes but I can't stand sitting still for hours every day. I get hyper and need to play ball. I rule the court." "I like music, I want to be like Jay Z." "Jay Z, come on, since when can you sing?" "I don't need to sing, I'll produce music like my cousin. And have beautiful women around me and you'll be begging to hang with me, Junior." "I want to be in charge and not have to listen to adults who think they know what's best for me. They are always telling you what you got to do different."

A quiet, studious member of the group waited until I singled him out and asked him. "I want to go to Harvard or Princeton."

I then asked what I thought was a natural follow up. How might they take their skills and interests and use them in the future as adults? Could they imagine ways to do this? I thought the question was generative and interesting. I was wrong. The question flopped and took all the air out of the room. The boys heard it as "What do you want to be when you grow up?" They dutifully responded, by rote, listing various professions.

My off-the-mark inquiry got me thinking more at length about how to help children become curious about and develop a language for their internal landscape, what enlivens them, what their life mission statement is, how they naturally move in the world. Of course, an understanding of these questions takes time to unfold. Even as adults, if we ask these questions, our answers change and evolve. But the skills to approach these explorations are best developed starting as young as possible!

These kinds of inquiries are not unlike the ones undertaken in my individual work with clients. I work in the same way with nine-year-olds as I do with eighty-year-olds. The language of exploration may be developmentally different for clients of different ages but the approach is the same.

Psychotherapy clients often come to this work because they are struggling.

Some are experiencing symptoms of depression or anxiety. Maybe they are having a crisis or radical shift in their life and want skills to navigate through it. As a clinician, I help them with tools to reduce painful and disruptive symptoms. But the method for the deep work of being present and shaping their lives is the same regardless of what brought them through the door.

Wouldn't it be amazing if this kind of exploration was not the purview of mindfulness retreats or some types of psychotherapies? The sooner we start to create a language and a method for understanding and developing our unique internal voices, the less likely we will be to hit a wall or have some sort of crisis motivate us to look more closely at our internal landscape.

Chapter 3

Distinguish Desire
from What Makes You Happy

There are two tragedies in life. One is to lose your heart's desire.
The other is to gain it.
George Bernard Shaw

What you desire and what makes you happy are often different. Standing in a realtor's window and having a momentary fantasy about an unaffordable dream home is not a problem. Nor is a fantasy about receiving accolades from someone you greatly admire. What gets you into trouble is when you are unaware of the amount of energy being directed toward your desires. That's the thing about objects of desire: They are easy to get lost in. Problems arise when you believe that fulfilling a desire will lead to an end of craving. When, in reality, it generally perpetuates it. Desires become a trap when you believe you are moving toward what will bring happiness and satisfaction and, instead, you are creating restlessness and dissatisfaction.

How Desire Can Trap You

Sebastian chaired an academic department. He had a longstanding habit of perceiving ways, real or imagined, that he was not respected. The desire to be respected and admired drove Sebastian to succeed. Wanting respect is natural, and it is deserved when we put our best efforts forward. A desire to be admired, though, often comes from not trusting our fundamental worthiness. In other words, we have to prove ourselves and receive external validation to experience ourselves as worthy. This was Sebastian's trap. In spite of having achieved respect from many, he continued to place disproportionate attention on those circumstances where he felt slighted.

Now with an awareness of how this deep-seated desire got in the way of his well-being, Sebastian felt discouraged that he had recently gotten riled up over a departmental event. John, a junior colleague, had held a meeting without him to strategize around achieving departmental goals. The goals had been established, in large part, by Sebastian. This was not a crucial meeting, nor was it the best use of Sebastian's time. John had even come to him with the meeting minutes for his feedback. Sebastian initially experienced this as a challenge to his authority and felt in a one-down position. He knew this feeling was irrational. While intellectually aware that he had asked John to assume increasing responsibility for meeting departmental goals, John's compliance left Sebastian feeling excluded and challenged. His craving for recognition left him feeling small.

In the room with me, Sebastian initially berated himself for feeling small. Getting down on himself for being caught in a desire trap did not help. By bringing self-compassion to desire traps, once they are recognized as a source of pain (because they are unquenchable) we are better able to get out of the trap. For Sebastian, bringing awareness to his self-judgment about his trap helped him create internal space, and he was then in a better position to let go of negative feelings.

With humor, Sebastian acknowledged, "I've begun to have some reasonable success at decreasing the number of damn meetings I have to go to! If I cut the number in half I could accomplish just as much and probably even more. And here I am being miserable that John was doing what I asked. Instead of recognizing that he is protecting my time, I viewed it as a personal affront."

Because Sebastian had an intentional practice of placing awareness on his internal response to what was happening, he was able to experience the irrational reactivity and let it pass without acting on it. Internally, though, he still reacted, feeling humbled as he shared with me the snarky comments to John that he had played out in his head.

Through intentional awareness practices, Sebastian could clearly see his experience as being in the grip of craving. He was trapped by a desire for a sense of importance and belonging that could not be fulfilled. He could not undo the painful past experiences in his life that helped create this trap, when he had felt belittled and dismissed. What he could do, now, was recognize when painful feelings from past experiences arose and distorted his perception of what was happening in the present moment.

With self-compassion Sebastian could now watch his perceptions and feelings around being slighted wash over without judging himself. By getting distance from his trap, he no longer saw his experience as a personal weakness.

The path to an intentional life requires an awareness of your desires as they are happening. There is no need to judge them. But try not to feed them. It isn't a problem to try to fulfill your desires. But how much energy and resources do they get? Can you see your desires for what they are, and recognize that they are temporary, whether or not they get fulfilled?

You may occasionally get trapped by your desires. By intentionally placing awareness on them as they arise, you can see them for what they are, putting them in healthy perspective rather than believing that fulfilling them will end craving or create happiness.

Which Types of Desire Pull You?

Desires can be pursued in both healthy and unhealthy ways. It is your relationship to the desire that is important to understand and develop practices around. Below are three categories of desires.

1. The desire for physical pleasures or material things is familiar to everyone. There is sometimes a fine line between a healthy pursuit of a desire and overvaluing it. If too many of your resources go toward fulfilling a desire, for example by chronic overwork, spending a lot of time thinking about material objects, or defining yourself by your sexual prowess, then you are prioritizing desires over experiences. Try to notice when passion or an appreciation for pleasure tips over into a craving.

2. There are desires to be something or someone we are not. I want to be fitter, more informed, more relevant, more patient, more whatever. You have to be careful of these desires because they can be mistaken for a healthy desire for self-improvement. These desires come from a position of being *not enough* and cannot be fulfilled. Perfectionism, the need to be perfect, is this type of desire. This is a trap because it encourages you to compare yourself to others, and even when you feel good enough, this situation is only temporary. The desire to be something other than you are inevitably leads to the dead end of looking outside yourself for validation.

3. Another desire that can trap you is the desire *to get away from*, to numb or blunt yourself. We can do this in many different ways: drugs, alcohol, food, video games, shopping, porn, oversleeping, overuse of social media. These desires come from an inability to look at or tolerate what is happening inside. Like the other desires, these can become compulsive or addictive, and physically take on a life of their own.

The desire for money deserves special mention because it actually represents different types of desires. For example, a preoccupation with money can be a fear of not having enough or being enough. It can be a desire for material wealth, recognition, pleasure, or validation. We live in a culture that can deify wealth in an unhealthy way, so it is easy to give it too much head space. This is perhaps why we are one of the wealthiest countries in the world while also one of the most stressed out, with climbing rates of anxiety and depression.

Some desires really do serve your highest nature, are in line with what matters most, and make you happy. For example: the desire to feel free, the desire to love and be loved, the desire to be generous, the desire to make a difference in the world.

Even with healthy higher-level desires, you can still get lost in desire traps. For example, imagine that you work for a non-profit for a cause you believe in deeply. You have taken a pay cut because the work is more in alignment with your core values. This job choice in the service of a higher-level desire does not stop you from craving recognition from others and feeling small when you don't get it. Another example: You have the desire to be generous with others, but fulfilling the desire is dependent on others admiring your generosity. Generosity not given freely, conditioned on admiration, becomes a trap. And still another example: You value practicing meditation or mindfulness, but it's important for you to be viewed as someone who is highly evolved. In this way, even meditation can become a trap.

When tremendous energy goes to fulfilling your desires, and you believe these desires will give you something more or deeper, you will feel restless and as if something is missing. Your awareness of all that is here, right now, is dimmed.

A healthy relationship to desires is to respect and enjoy them, open to them without getting lost in them. Give them some energy without giving them too much of yourself. You don't need to act on every desire in order to open to them. Denying desire is also unhealthy because they are a natural part of being in your body. Allowing room for desires, with an intention to understand them and their impact, leads to a greater understanding of yourself. In an intentional life, desires are enjoyed without being chased. They aren't confused with what brings lasting happiness.

Chasing Desire: Blind to the Forest Through the Trees

Pam grew up a "good girl," a straight-A student who listened to her parents. She craved her father's approval but couldn't remember ever having received it. She learned from a young age to take care of her mother's emotional needs. Striving to do everything right was her characteristic style in childhood. When she got to college, she experienced herself as a completely different person, partying heavily and feeling empowered by being both sexual and sexually desired.

Pam's desire became a trap because, while she did enjoy being sexually free, she was unaware that what she really longed for was the experience of being special to someone. She didn't give this much conscious thought and assumed someday she'd meet the right person for her and settle down. Yet an unexamined belief was thwarting her happiness. This belief was that she would never meet someone who would love her just as she was.

Now in her thirties, Pam wondered why she wasn't meeting anyone she found special who found her special in return. She was still chasing physical desire as a form of connection, hoping it would lead to deeper intimacy. Of course, Pam's enjoyment of her sexuality wasn't interfering with her relationship aspirations, but her approach to desire was. She often drank heavily on first dates and enjoyed sexual banter with someone she just recently met. By mixing up desire with a longing to meaningfully connect, Pam was unconsciously perpetuating her belief that the men she was interested in desired her sexually but did not wish to pursue a more significant relationship.

By placing awareness on her desires and how she pursued them, Pam understood how she conflated desire with deeper connection, and how doing so left her frustrated and increasingly hopeless.

In contrast to Pam's romantic life, she approached friendships in ways that led to rich connections and deep bonds. These same skills extended to colleagues and clients where she felt valued. In these relationships, Pam was open without giving too much away. She initially presented her best self and left others curious to know more. She was more judicious about how she revealed herself. Being judicious is different from being guarded.

Pam was able to engage in a healthy and skillful relationship dance when she saw herself as worthy just as she was. Understanding this, she reflected on ways to take the same skills she brought to her friendships to her dating life. As a result, she became more discerning and approached dating with greater confidence. Her desires organically shifted: she had less desire to drink heavily on dates and found men who appreciated her strengths more attractive. This shift in relationship to her own desires was more in line with a belief of being worthy of deeper connection. Not surprisingly, the quality of her dates changed and Pam knew she was moving in the direction of more meaningful connection.

The Dalai Lama speaks of practicing contentment as an antidote to the pain and suffering caused by craving and unfulfillable desires. Implied in the words *practicing contentment* is active choice. It is an active choice to recognize all you have right now and to believe that you are enough and that you have enough. Practicing contentment makes room for opening up to having things that are not here now while still partaking in the abundance of the present.

Exercise: Bring Greater Awareness to What You Desire

Where do your desire traps lie? Money, recognition, power? Do you sometimes use food, alcohol, or drugs as a way to get distance from what is happening? Do you spend a lot of time thinking about what you would do with money you don't have? Do you play out scenarios of people rejecting or criticizing you? Or fantasize about people showering you with admiration and praise?

Write down a desire that has been a trap for you. You might refer to the list of different types of desires earlier in the chapter, such as desire for pleasure-seeking or material things, to be other than you are, or to use things as a means to get away from discomfort. Do any of those desires tip over into traps?

For each desire you write down, create an intentional practice around it and implement it in the coming weeks. For example, if you spend lots of time thinking about how to make more money, can you notice yourself doing this as it is happening and consciously redirect your awareness back to the present moment? Can you stop checking your online investments more than is needed to wisely manage them? Or, another example, if you enjoy getting high at the end of the day, can you choose another way to practice relaxation? If a craving to get high comes up, can you watch it come and go without acting on it?

Chapter 4

The Benefits of Pausing
and Stillness

*In an age of constant movement, nothing is
so urgent as sitting still.*
Pico Iyer

To meaningfully shape your life, learn to pause. Pausing is stepping back
from thinking and habitual ways of doing, and simply noticing. Pausing
is the entryway to stillness, in body and mind. Practicing pausing and valuing stillness is the doorway to all contemplative practices. It is in stillness
that you most intimately know yourself. Pausing, and the quiet and stillness
that comes with it, is initially uncomfortable. It becomes comfortable, and
desirable, as you witness its transformative powers.

Pausing is not typically a first response. A more typical initial response
is to think, to do, to act. It is part of our biology to want to *do something*.
We have characteristic, often unhelpful, ways of coping with what makes us
uncomfortable: like ignoring it, distracting ourselves, fleeing from it, prematurely analyzing it, denying it, and blaming others for it. Jumping to habitual
ways of handling discomfort, rather than pausing and opening to stillness,

prevents a clear understanding of what is happening. These habits to deal with discomfort actually make it worse. Pausing lets you become aware of these habits as they are happening. This is the first step to being able to do things differently.

Building your capacity for pausing, and opening to the stillness within it, you learn skillful means to cope with discomfort. This leads to the greatest freedom of choice and action.

When I want to be away from my internal discomfort, I try to recall a quote by John Burroughs, the nineteenth-century naturalist. "Do not despise your own place and hour. Every place is under the stars, every place is the center of the world." These words help me pause and stay with what is happening right now, even when I don't like it.

Pausing is a Foundation of Mindfulness

Enrica was a striking young woman who knew that she was attractive and intelligent. She had a healthy appreciation for herself, and yet this positive regard was in stark contrast to her habit of reproaching herself for laziness and other small inadequacies. Enrica believed self-criticism motivated her to try harder and be better. She was unaware of the cost to her well-being of not accepting herself as she was.

Most of the time Enrica's self-reproach was a quiet stream in the background of her awareness. However, when she felt uncertain or was having a difficult time, her self-criticism became louder and overwhelmed her. At these times, she sought comfort in binge eating. Binge eating didn't comfort her—it numbed her. When she binged, it was as if she emotionally left the room, compartmentalizing her pain outside of her awareness. Compartmentalizing pain doesn't address it. As a result, binge eating intensified Enrica's pain. She was filled with self-loathing the day after binging.

After a few sessions, Enrica told me, "I keep telling myself that I can't have what I want. I'm constantly down on myself, telling myself I'm not good enough or I'm lazy. Or whatever happens to be the self-repercussion of the day. I knew I thought this way but didn't know how frequently I thought this way. It's kind of shocking. But I can't imagine doing it differently. How do I do that?"

My response to a statement like this ("I now see what I'm doing that hurts me or holds me back, now what?!") is to highlight the insight that came from the pause and the feeling of urgency to do something about it. I focus on what an accomplishment it is simply to notice what is happening as it is happening. It is a big deal to tolerate the discomfort that is present without jumping into action or resorting to habitual responses. It is so important that you not gloss over what you notice about your thoughts and perceptions, and your physical responses. Enrica, understandably, wanted to jump from noticing what was happening to doing something about it. Before doing something about it, she first needed to find ways to care for herself within the discomfort, rather than run from or react to it.

Pausing and noticing are the doorways to your capacity to practice mindful reflection. They are the bedrock of real freedom to make choices and take action that lead to meaningful and lasting change.

How do you begin to feel more comfortable with pausing, especially with discomfort? Practice noticing without judging, and noticing without immediately looking for deeper implications. Simply noticing. Easier said than done. Simply noticing is often far from simple. And yet pausing in difficult experiences presents the kernel for radically transforming them.

Enrica's practice of bringing awareness to her habit of self-reproach enabled her to change the way she spoke to herself. Talking to herself with kindness, rather than judgment, changed the way she felt. Enrica brought this heightened conscious awareness to moments when she was uncertain and in pain. She came to trust she could tolerate these moments, face them, and be OK. This realization was empowering and her confidence grew. This awareness helped Enrica to face, rather than compartmentalize, painful experiences and she eventually stopped using food as a way of closing herself off from her internal experience.

The practice of pausing and noticing what is happening offers you alternate ways of moving through discomfort. Naturally and organically, you

develop healthier options for allowing room for all of your experience, including discomfort.

The answers that come to you out of pausing, and stillness, are more creative and effective than suggestions someone else can give. Yes, sometimes you need help from others. Still, simply pausing and noticing what is happening inside lets you see unhelpful habits for what they are. Their power becomes reduced. Pausing quiets down your struggle against discomfort and allows your inherent wisdom to come to the fore.

Exercise: Simply Noticing is an Important Pause

Walk around the block with an intention simply to notice. You might first notice what comes to you visually. You might then notice subtler things like the experience of your body as you are walking: the sensation of your feet touching the ground, the sensation of the breeze as it touches your face, moves your hair or rustles your clothes. You might notice the smells on the street: exhaust, food from store fronts, fresh air. Notice what you do with the smells. Can you let them come and go? Notice the differences in your response to smells you find pleasant and those you don't. Notice the sounds: birds, car radios, engines, people talking. Notice the absence of sounds and the alteration between near and distant sounds. Notice the natural ebb and flow of a particular sound.

As you notice this panoply of stimuli, you will likely associate to what you notice, or get distracted and think about the day's activities, or find some mental scape other than the one right here. This practice is to bring yourself back, again and again, to what you notice while walking.

If this relatively non-emotionally laden task challenges your ability to stay present, imagine trying to stay present to things when you are emotionally triggered, stressed, or very invested in a certain outcome. Imagine the challenge of simply noticing, without interfering, when it comes to moving toward your long-term goals and highest aspirations.

The Anxiety of Never Being Still

Jamie was a young man who came to therapy for help with pervasive, and at times paralyzing, anxiety. He felt pressure to be more successful and did not know whether to stay in the restaurant industry or change career paths entirely. Jamie heard I worked with hypnosis and on his first visit to me for therapy challenged me to hypnotize him: "I don't think I can be hypnotized." Interested in why he thought this, he explained, "I am so stressed, I can't relax! I don't even know how to unwind when I go to sleep. I don't unwind, I stay wired until I just pass out. There's no way you can talk to me that will put me in a relaxed state!" What was interesting was not whether Jamie could go into a state of therapeutic trance but, instead, that he never experienced himself as relaxed.

Knowing that Jamie recently began taking yoga classes, I asked him how he experienced the final relaxation, the end of class when you lie down and physical movement postures are over. Here, the focused awareness of the postures and breath cease, and you let go of any effort. This part of the class is important because the nervous system relaxes, allowing the body and mind to integrate the physical practices of the past hour. Jamie's feeling about this "relaxing" part of the class was, not surprisingly, "I hate it! I want to get the hell out of there!"

The work in therapy with Jamie initially focused on building pauses into his day and coping with the discomfort of being still. This was done in two ways. First, by setting aside time to move his body, because the only time Jamie experienced a calm mind was when he ran. I encouraged him to build in time to run most days and to protect that time. The second type of pause was to notice when his mind jumped ahead, which was constantly. When he noticed his "jumping ahead mind," he was to try to bring himself back to the present moment. This type of pausing was the most foreign and difficult for Jamie. Importantly, he committed to trying.

His efforts to step back from his habit of jumping ahead helped Jamie see, in a way he never had, how his aversion to stillness undermined his ability to make effective choices—to even know his preferences. He had to be present to his experiences to be able to evaluate them. Jamie's habit of constantly doing, his mind's endless jumping around and ahead, was creating a state of constant unease and anxiety.

As Jamie strengthened his ability to pause, he still had the impulse to flee from stillness. But he also increasingly tolerated the experience of pausing and noticing. He built up, very gradually, the ability to slow down. In the pauses, Jamie noticed the micro-moments when he desired to flee and, in fact, often still did flee. What changed for him was that he also built up the capacity to bring himself back to moments of stillness. These moments of coming back to the present accumulated and gradually began to change his experience. He became less anxious and gained confidence in his ability to make decisions that would eventually help him craft a career that matched his skills and interests.

Jamie kept up with yoga practice and when I last saw him, the final relaxation was still his least favorite part of the class. However, he recognized its importance and, occasionally, enjoyed it.

Even if we don't relate to Jamie's particular experience, if we are honest we can identify our own challenges to pausing and being still. Most of us can relate to wanting "to get the hell out of" an experience, whether by distracting ourselves, zoning out, or finding something else *to do*.

Stepping Back from Routine and In-the-Moment Pausing

What does the practice of pausing concretely look like? It is helpful to conceptualize two types of pausing practices. The first type of pause is to

step back, in action, from your daily routine. This kind of practice can occur in breaks throughout the day or for longer chunks of time. The second type of pause, subtler, is to notice what is happening as it happens. The first type of pause helps to develop the transformative, in-the-moment, second type.

The purpose of the first kind of pause is to step back from routine. This kind of pause can be any activity where you step back from your routine and your habits of mind. Earlier in the chapter, Jamie did this by incorporating running into his schedule as a way of quieting his thoughts. Vacations and travel to new places can do this. Other kinds of pausing are: occasionally leaving work early to do something you enjoy or walking around the block in the middle of a work day; turning off your phone for an hour or more a day; practicing yoga; taking naps; getting a massage; writing in a journal; meditation; sitting in nature; physical exercise; listening to music.

This first kind of pause has the quality of engagement, not distraction. This is important because there are countless ways to distract ourselves. For example, how much time in a day do you spend internet surfing? Facebook relies on our attention being pulled away from the present moment in order to generate advertising revenue. It is fine to occasionally take a break and watch a television show, play a video game, text, or internet surf. This is not, however, pausing in an intentional way and does not promote a centering stillness.

You probably do try to incorporate the first type of pause into your life. What is important is that you schedule and honor the time set aside for these pauses. Don't let the obligations of everyday life intrude on them.

The second kind of pause, the practice of noticing what is happening as it is happens, is the heart of mindfulness practices. I'll refer to it here as the Mindful Pause. The first kind of pause (quieting down through stepping back from routine in ways that cultivate engagement) is in the service of the Mindful Pause. For example, if you meditate, it is not because it is inherently noble but because it helps you pause and stay present to all aspects of daily life as you are living it. The Mindful Pause, and the stillness it brings, holds the key to accessing your internal resources and developing your most authentic self.

The Mindful Pause can be done in diverse ways. Earlier in the chapter Jamie learned to watch his attention as it jumped beyond the present moment, an important Mindful Pause. He tried to bring his awareness back to the present moment, another important pause practice. Here are just a few other examples of the Mindful Pause. If you sit all day at your desk, every so often stand up and notice the sensations in your body. Drink a cup of coffee or tea and be aware of your sensory experience as you take each and every sip. When you are angry and want to lash out, touch your heart and say to yourself in a kind voice, "Anger". When you are under a tight deadline, take time to notice how you are experiencing the pressure—dip below the thoughts and notice your body. Walk around the block, you have time for it! When you are responding to an email, can you pause and stay present to just that one email rather than focusing on multiple things at once? When you are half listening to someone while thinking of something else, pause and bring yourself back to the conversation at hand.

One of the most helpful pausing practices is to anchor yourself in your breath. Throughout the day, step back from what you are doing and place your full attention on the inhale and exhale of your breath for at least thirty seconds.

Consistently practice pausing. Practice every day and throughout the day. This sounds simple, and yet it is a radically different approach to how we often go through our days.

When you practice the second kind of in-the-moment pausing, recognize it! Especially notice those moments when you have stepped back from habitual ways of perceiving, thinking, and acting. Building up your capacity to automatically pause more of the time has the transformational benefit of centering you; tapping into your internal resources no matter what is happening around you.

Exercise: A Valuable Practice of Pausing and Breathing

Try this exercise twice a day for a month. It only takes a few minutes and offers tremendous benefits if you stay with it. Until this practice becomes a natural part of your day, schedule it! Find a relatively quiet place to practice.

To start, either close your eyes or pick a point a few feet in front of you to comfortably direct your gaze. Then take five easy, full breaths and place your awareness on each in-breath and out-breath.

After the five breaths are finished, shift your awareness to all that is happening inside you. Notice the physical sensations. Watch them come and watch them go. Notice thoughts that arise. Don't chase them or push them away. Watch them come and watch them go. Notice if feelings come up, or the experience of comfort and discomfort. Watch the feelings and experiences come and go. Stay in this stillness for a full two minutes. As this practice becomes familiar, your internal clock will know when two minutes have passed. After two minutes, take a couple more breaths, allowing your attention to extend to the room. Return to your day with the freshness of having paused and tapped into your interior resources.

Deep work in psychotherapy comes out of the pauses in the room. I work with clients to help them stay present to whatever arises in the pauses, which are often initially uncomfortable. They understandably want a way to conceptualize their difficulties, for example, through interpretation. And they want to do something. While these strategies are sometimes helpful, the deepest insights are borne out of the stillness of the pause. Together we give these moments the attention and care they deserve. I give them feedback on their pausing as well as on ways they try to move away from stillness. I offer ways to deepen the pause and encourage them to notice what comes out of it. This process is very empowering. What arises from their stillness holds more insight, utility, and truth than any expert opinion.

Helping Children Pause: The Younger the Better

As with most intentional practices, pausing can be done at any age. Helping children learn to pause provides them with an invaluable foundation for skillfully navigating their lives.

Nathan was a bright nine-year old who, at this young age, believed that getting down on himself motivated him to do better. He was so articulate about his internal world that it was easy to forget that he was, developmentally, still a nine-year-old. He had challenges regulating negative feelings and they got him into trouble at home and school. Angry outbursts were often followed by remorse. Nathan did not initially understand my encouragement to try to find ways to express his feelings differently while also having compassion for himself when he felt out of control. Like many adults, he felt he was either justified or to blame for his anger. He had difficulty discerning the feeling from the expression of the feeling.

I also met with Nathan's mother to explore ways they could practice intention together. One recent evening they were playing Uno, a card game, before he went to bed. In Uno, you try to match the color or number in the discard pile and a player must pick up a card if he cannot discard. The first person to get rid of all her cards sticks the other players with points. When the game began, Nathan accumulated a disproportionate number of blue cards and angrily announced, "Oh no, every time I begin Uno with blue cards I lose!" Nathan's mother gently replied, "Really Nathan? The game just started. You really believe the blue cards are that bad?"

Nathan then said in a new way, "Reminds me of what Lisa tells me, that it's easier for me to see the bad things about me than the good things."

Nathan's mom was also practicing pausing before talking, using less words to help Nathan become more receptive to what she says. Well-placed words guide kids while still allowing them to have their own experience. A good rule of thumb for teaching moments with kids: Less is more! Nathan's mom resisted the urge to use Nathan's insight during Uno as an opportunity to provide a longer lesson. Instead, she witnessed Nathan's important insight. She said simply and effectively, "Good noticing Nathan, I'm impressed. Maybe it doesn't have to be that way?" The Uno game continued. She heightened the impact of Nathan's insight that came out of his ability to pause, by reinforcing it and admiring it, and him.

This is the pause-in-action, the second kind of pausing practice. Building on these moments—again and again—is the foundation for transformation, the foundation of living intentionally.

Chapter 5

The Fundamentals of Awareness: Openness and Constriction

Your hand opens and closes and opens and closes. If it were always a fist or always stretched open, you would be paralyzed. Your deepest presence is in every small contracting and expanding, the two as beautifully balanced and coordinated as bird wings.

Rumi

You are always alternating between states of openness and constriction. These physical states are most often unconscious responses, as automatic as breathing. States of openness and constriction are the foundations of thoughts, perceptions, motivations, preferences, choices, and action. This basic, mostly pre-verbal, level of responding is your body's intelligent animal nature.

There is a deep-seated, inaccurate belief in Western culture that the mind is the brain. But the mind is embodied, both body and brain. Dualism leads to overvaluing disembodied thought, and as a result, cognitions are cut off from a critical knowledge source. Thought that is disconnected from the wisdom of the body is as likely to be a source of conflict and misunderstanding as it is a source of problem-solving and understanding.

To understand yourself at the deepest level, practice dipping below your thoughts and become a watchful student of your body's states of openness and constriction. Establishing an intentional practice of placing awareness on the many ways you are open and closed (i.e., constricted), as it is happening, is fundamental to knowing yourself.

Lydia was the only woman on the executive committee in her company. She had difficulty allowing herself to be genuine and shine in her role. She generally felt supported by her male colleagues, but also sensed that they shared an ease and style of communicating with each other that they didn't share with her. This made it even more challenging for her to try to bring greater authenticity to the way she worked.

As Lydia told me about feeling contained in her role at work, she held her arms closely to her sides and she spoke quietly and evenly, without animation. She expressed a strong desire to break out, to no longer contain herself, and didn't want to care so much about how she would be perceived by colleagues. As Lydia set her intention to work toward this goal, she began to take risks and allowed greater spontaneity in her interactions with colleagues. She showed her witty, dry humor with less self-consciousness about how it would be received.

As Lydia told me about the changes within herself and how they manifested at work, the physical constrictions in the way she held herself tightly in the therapy office also changed. She began to laugh, even occasionally guffawing. When she laughed her face looked younger and animated. Now she told me work stories with her hands moving fluidly in front of her. The movement of her arms reflected the growing expansiveness she was feeling. Lydia raised her voice in enthusiasm and allowed herself to tell me about her substantial strengths. She even transformed the way she dressed, now with her own unique signature. She became more interested in being herself than fitting in at work.

Lydia's transformation at work from constriction to greater openness, from the "odd man out" to uniquely herself, had parallels in body language. And as I noticed changes, I pointed them out. Lydia learned to use her body's language to gain important feedback. She sometimes consciously let her body movements lead her, enjoying the process of taking up more space in her role at work.

The more you are open, the happier you are. By placing awareness on your states of both openness and constriction—knowing yourself on this intimate level—you are at your most authentic. You know yourself so well that you feel safe and comfortable most of the time, which enables you to stay open more of the time. You trust your capacity to protect yourself when you need to. In alignment with your true nature, joining with the wisdom of your body, you are comfortable showing yourself to others. This comfort with yourself is, in return, met with greater openness by others. In fact, by understanding yourself at this subtle, nonverbal level, you become skilled at finding environments that facilitate being open and undefended. When this happens, you can masterfully shape your life.

It is not that you are always open to experience. This is neither possible nor desirable. Constrictions serve a protective function. For example, you constrict when you are cautious and in self-defense. This is as adaptive for the human animal as it is for every animal. You constrict in quiet ways when you are hesitant, for example, when testing out a new experience like learning to drive or ski. Sometimes you constrict when you are preparing for a challenge, such as the nerves you experience before a big exam.

Constriction only becomes problematic when you habitually approach new experiences by constricting when it isn't necessary. Thoughts and beliefs, as well as lifestyle, can present challenges to cultivating open states. For example, when you are overstressed and overcommitted, you don't have the reserves to stay open, so you are more likely to meet experience out of an impatient (constricted) place. If you are suspicious of others' motives (constriction), you are unlikely to find a way to way to collaborate with others (openness) to create solutions to problems. When you have been hurt in the past and have not let go of the hurt, or perhaps have not learned how to healthfully protect yourself, you are more likely to approach new experiences out of a fearful (constricted) place. When you constrict out of habit, it limits your capacity to meet new experiences from a creative, adaptive place.

Become an expert observer of your physical experience of openness and constriction. Befriend the wisdom of your body. Often by the time you respond cognitively, emotionally, and behaviorally to physical opening and constriction, the opportunity to track them at their physical source is long past. If you want to understand your thoughts, your motivations, and your preferences, then come to know your body's response on this subtle level. The body often points the way to what is happening in a more direct way than your thoughts do. You just need to learn the language of your body.

The Experience of Openness and Constriction

States of openness are often experienced as pleasurable or positive experiences. States of constriction are often experienced as discomfort or negative experiences. However, this is not always the case.

These are examples of the experience of open states: curiosity, connection, happiness, joy, peaceful, inspired, patient, expansive, moved, generous, tender, excited (can also be constricted), confident, empathic, grateful, and compassionate.

These are examples of the experience of constriction: aversion, rage, weariness, feeling stuck, anxiety, repulsion, anger (can also be open), holding back, shame, confusion, inhibition, fear, suspicion, doubt, embarrassment, annoyance, struggle, and pain.

Again, all of these experiences have physiological correlates. Imagine experiences when you felt one or more of the states listed above. How did you experience these states in your body? As you practice placing awareness on physical states of openness and constriction, you will become clearer on the connection between the physical sensations and the felt experience. You will be able to watch the thoughts and stories that arise from these states. With time, you can learn to positively influence your response to these physical states.

Openness and constriction can be experienced side by side. Have you enjoyed a haunted house in your childhood? Or a roller coaster? There is an experience of excited and anxious anticipation as you round a corner waiting for someone to jump out at you, or as your car pauses at the top of the tracks ready to plummet downward with the force of gravity.

Emotions can be experienced with both openness and constriction. For example, anger is often experienced as aversive (constriction). Yet it can also be an emotion that energizes you to act on your own behalf, like speaking up when you are being treated with disrespect. If handled with skill, anger can lead to an opening and deepening of experience. It can lead to your demanding respect and removing yourself from conditions that don't serve your well-being. However, when anger causes you to shut down, feel helpless, or to lash out reactively, it perpetuates a constricted experience and does not lead to well-being. You may feel temporary relief at telling someone off or imagining punching them in the nose, but those expressions of anger generally come from internal states of constriction and a limited view of yourself. Those responses keep you small (constricted) internally.

Sadness, like anger, is an emotion that can be experienced both as openness and constriction. Learning to open to any state which arises makes all your experience informative and potentially helpful.

Have you ever belted out a song or danced with abandon believing no one was looking or listening? Then you found out that you were being watched and suddenly felt a little embarrassed? This is an experience of great openness moving into a small constriction. If you felt shame, you experienced a big constriction. Or maybe you were in a large group of people listening to an inspiring speaker and during the question and answer period you were moved to raise your hand (openness). You weren't chosen right away and as time passed you began to wonder whether your question was a good one and got a little nervous (constriction).

How to Be Skillful with Your Constrictions

While open states are associated to positive feelings and a sense of well-being, constrictions can be adaptive too. For example, it is helpful to avoid a potentially unhealthy or dangerous situation. If you are walking down the street and a dog barks at you, and you don't know this dog's signals or sense of safety in the world, it is wise to give the dog space as you walk by. If you witness an escalating argument between two people that is becoming aggressive, it is adaptive to steer clear. If someone who has a history of talking badly about people tries to engage you in conversation about someone, the weariness you feel is helpful information.

Many times, though, we constrict when there is no clear danger. For example, this can happen when you experience negative emotions as so uncomfortable that you push them out of your awareness. The problem with this as a habitual response is that you end up cutting off the experience in order to get away from what is painful or uncomfortable. When you do this, you limit experience by missing the opportunity to explore what is happening and learn from it. You might communicate unconsciously to yourself that you are not safe or that you do not know how to take care of yourself in the situation. You might learn to avoid what feels bad but then miss an opportunity to see how resourceful and adaptive you can be.

It is important not to ignore constrictions but, rather, be curious about them. Ignoring constrictions can lead to acting against your well-being. When things don't work out well because you didn't listen to your body's messages, it is often too late to go back and learn from the wisdom of the body. By ignoring constrictions, they are likely to be expressed as shutting down or reactivity, rather than skillful reflection and action.

There's a difference between how you consciously notice your constrictions and how they occur in your body. Because they are lightning-fast, they are often not accessible to cognition or language. Still, with practice noticing the experience of constriction that is accessible to your conscious awareness, you will develop insights about yourself; insights that will improve both the quality of your reflections and your capacity to make good decisions and take effective action.

By bringing curiosity to constrictions, they become less aversive. This lets you discover when constrictions contain a source of wisdom, when they come from unwarranted fears, and when they are a combination of the two. By opening to these experiences, you learn to approach challenging situations in novel and adaptive ways.

Exercise: Change the Quality of Your Constrictions

This exercise is meant to help you practice creating space (openness) around the experience of both physical and emotional constriction. Practicing releasing around physical constriction is helpful when working with difficult emotions.

Clench several parts of your body tightly; each part separately. Your face, your shoulders, and your stomach. Starting with your face, clench it tight for a few seconds—then release it. Do this three times. Notice how it feels when you are clenching and when you release. After you have done this, move onto your shoulders. Shrug them tightly, then release. And then move onto your stomach. You now have a good model of how you can creatively practice opening around difficult emotions.

Imagine a time you were annoyed or upset during the past few weeks. It doesn't have to have been a major event. For example, were you on hold with poor customer service? Did someone cut you off while driving? Did you feel excluded? Vividly imagine this event and how you experienced the constriction in your body. Once you have it vividly in your mind, imagine bringing openness to the experience. In this exercise, you might imagine the actual experience of annoyance or anger changing as you open to it.

Tracking the Moment-to-Moment Dance of the Body

Lena came to therapy because she was holding back from taking risks in areas that were important to her. She gave a good deal of thought to things she wanted to do and steps she wanted to take toward her interests, but she had difficulty translating these thoughts into action. Early into our work, in spite of her fears, she stood up for herself at work in a way that surprised her. At her yearly review, she presented the case to her boss about why she was a good candidate for a new position that required leadership and more responsibility. When her boss spoke candidly about Lena's tendency to not take initiative (i.e., holding herself back), Lena was able to acknowledge her boss's concerns while also clearly explaining how she was making strides to be more open and assertive. After this frank and honest dialogue, her boss agreed that Lena was a good candidate for the position.

Following this conversation with her boss Lena came to a psychotherapy session beaming, expansive, and excited (openness). I noticed her glow and enthusiasm and it was contagious (my openness). I commented on how she was glowing and Lena looked away shyly (small constriction). Since speaking on behalf of herself was a relatively new experience for Lena, I asked her to tell me more about it. As she began to talk, she began second-guessing herself, wondering if her boss found her to be too full of herself (doubt-constriction). Here, in the open space of exploration between us, Lena quickly became uncomfortable with her internal state of expansiveness and confidence. She may also have been uncomfortable celebrating herself with me and allowing me to celebrate her. This became the focus of what was happening. Instead of exploring the familiar self-doubt in the face of possibility (which was important but already very familiar to her) I asked her if she could allow this uncertainty, and more importantly, allow the excitement and possibility that had been in the room between us just moments ago. She said, shyly (ever so slight constriction), that she would try (an important opening).

This is a great example because it shows that while openness is associated with positive experiences, it can also lead to constriction when the experience is new and frightening. Even more importantly, it is an example of how allowing the experience of constriction, and opening into it, can actually change the experience of constriction. If Lena had gone down the familiar path of exploring her experience of doubt, she likely would have missed the opportunity to experience firsthand how she could stay with the constriction in her body and open up to a different experience, the kind of new experience she so wanted to welcome into her life.

Lena's willingness to give more room to the expansive experience ushered in yet another important new experience. A tender sadness (openness) welled up in her. Sadness arose when she recognized her lifelong habit of keeping herself small, and incorrectly believing that this small state protected her. With this sadness came a recognition, a kind of declaration, that keeping herself small was no longer acceptable (prelude to big openness). Here the sadness is a lovely openness because it has the quality of kindness and self-compassion. The sadness held the kernel of possibility of wanting, and choosing, to let herself shine.

How to Infuse Openness Into All Experience

The intentional practice of meeting difficult emotions with openness makes the experience less painful and constricting. In fact, meeting all experience with openness can transform the experience. How do you bring openness to a constricted experience? You do so by inviting curiosity and compassion; by physically moving your body; by placing your hand on your heart when you are struggling; and by taking risks and being bold. Be creative! Every day, practice placing your awareness on the internal states of openness and constriction. Reflect upon what, if anything, you might do to infuse openness to all experience.

With an increased awareness of the many ways you experience openness and constriction, you'll discover ways you can influence your experience on these subtle levels. You'll discover you have more choice in your range of responses. You don't stop constricting, but you feel more open and at ease in general. You are more interested in creating conditions of openness and recognize that you can do this. For example, cooperating with others becomes more interesting than competing with them. Even when you constrict around anger, you recognize it is in your power to handle the experience skillfully. And things that don't go smoothly are less likely to evoke the same level of reactivity. As you become open more often, you feel conflict less often, and your effort and energy can be better directed in ways that serve your best interests.

Part II

Reflecting

Chapter 6

You Aren't Your Thoughts
(Unless You Think You Are)

We are dying from overthinking. We are slowly killing ourselves by thinking about everything. Think. Think. Think. You can never trust the human mind anyway.
Anthony Hopkins

W here your thoughts go, your energy follows. Where you place your energy influences your attention, which influences your choices, actions, and your life's direction. Intentional reflection is central to consciously shaping your life.

There are two areas of intentional practices that help train thought to serve your aspirations. The first, explored earlier in the chapter on pausing and creating stillness, are the practices that help calm and center the mind. The second type of reflection practice is wise investigation. This type of reflection is consciously choosing what to train your thoughts on as you ground your mind in reflection. Wise investigation is direct reflection. It amounts to a small proportion of actual time spent in thought. Intentional, direct reflection has the quality of open, ongoing consideration with an aim to deepen and widen understanding. It is the heart of creative and generative thought.

Become Conscious of the Quality & Content of Your Thoughts

David Bohm, a renowned twentieth-century quantum physicist who also wrote about the nature of the mind, recognized that the way we think—which can solve the most complex problems—is also the source of our most significant problems. *Sustained incoherence* was his term for the way our thoughts often cover up what is really happening.

> *"Thought runs you. Thought, however, gives false info that you are running it, that you are the one that controls thought. Whereas actually thought is the one which controls each of us. Thought is creating divisions out of itself and then saying that they are there naturally. This is another major feature of thought: Thought doesn't know it is doing something and then it struggles against what it is doing. It doesn't want to know that it is doing it. And thought struggles against the results; trying to avoid those unpleasant results while keeping on with that way of thinking."*

We don't often recognize just how noisy our thoughts are. They operate like a soundtrack in the background of the mind. While this may sound benign, they pull attention away from what is here in the present moment. Noisy thoughts interfere with the capacity to focus attention and directly reflect.

Understanding when thoughts are helpful, when they are neutral but taking up too much space, and when they are unhelpful is a core intentional practice in reflection. Practice placing awareness on the nature of your thoughts, both their quality and content, as they are occurring, in order to understand how they function for you. You are not at the mercy of your thoughts.
Differentiating the thoughts that clarify and deepen understanding from the those that are habitual, noisy, and unhelpful is an essential skill to develop.

When you notice the nature of your thinking, the goal is not to control your thoughts. That isn't possible. When you witness how often your thoughts take you away from being fully present, you will likely become less enamored with them. Becoming less attached to thoughts helps quiet them. The practice of witnessing your thoughts, and gaining distance from them, helps bring you back to being present.

Making your thoughts more conscious does not mean spending even more time and energy on them. It generally means the opposite. Though as with all new practices, it initially requires effortful attention in order to become skilled at watching thoughts as you are having them. The practice includes noticing which types of thoughts are compelling, even engaging, but don't add to your life. These thoughts aren't a problem when in moderation. Obviously, not all thought needs to be helpful or serve some purpose. But it is tremendously important to observe when you put too much energy into thoughts that do not serve the purpose that you believe they serve.

As thinking becomes more conscious, it is not that you can control your thoughts, but rather, unhelpful thoughts don't have as much power over you. Over time, when you witness them *as they are occurring*, the nature and quality of your thoughts actually change. Thoughts quiet down and, because they do, are more helpful and informative.

What Is Helpful and Unhelpful Thinking?

Because your thoughts come from you, bringing awareness to them enables you to gradually influence them. Increasing the percentage of helpful to unhelpful thoughts is transformative.

Thoughts can be helpful or unhelpful in both content and quality. There are individual differences in styles of thinking, each with their own strengths and challenges. For example, some people are big picture, expansive thinkers. Others are pragmatic, present goal-oriented thinkers. Appreciating other thinking styles can promote a broader perspective and more flexible thought.

Every one of us engages in unhelpful thinking, probably much of the time! For example, it is impossible to not be biased in thought. But, with skillful reflection, you can try to bring consciousness to how bias impacts your thinking.

In general, thoughts that stem from direct observation are helpful. Other examples of helpful thoughts include: thoughts that reveal and challenge your underlying assumptions; thoughts from an open internal state; critical but non-judgmental thought; thoughts that reflect upon your personal core values; thought focused on helpful questions; uncluttered thought; curious thinking; thoughts about what you don't know; reflective thoughts on the ideas of others (receptive thought); focused thinking on values or big-question thoughts; connecting ideas in new ways thoughts; earnest self-inquiry thoughts; non-distracted thoughts.

When the mind is constantly thinking as a habit, it is unhelpful. In this state, even potentially helpful thoughts get lost because there is so much background noise. Other examples of unhelpful thoughts are: either/or thinking; overgeneralizing thoughts; unconscious bias; anxious and fearful thoughts; jumping to conclusions thoughts; judgmental thinking; rigid thinking; trying-to-be-right thoughts; racing and repetitive thoughts; overvaluing thought thoughts.

You can't dictate how your thoughts arise. But as you practice noticing them and making them more conscious, you are in a better position to choose how much energy you give them. You can consciously choose to give unhelpful thoughts less importance, limiting their power over you. Through direct reflection, you can train your mind to spend more energy on helpful thoughts that help you make better choices and take more effective action.

With all this thinking about thinking, it is hard to imagine how this helps to decrease unhelpful thinking! Paradoxically, as you get clearer on the nature and quality of your thoughts, you'll understand how you need to think less in order to know more.

When your thoughts quiet down, you can guide them to be more helpful. Practice placing more attention on helpful thoughts, increasing the ratio of helpful to non-helpful thoughts. Be patient and persistent. Build up your capacity to consciously pause and notice the quality of thoughts as you are having them. And when you do, highlight this awareness. These moments are worthy of your attention.

Thoughts impact your mood and your mood impacts your thoughts. It is a bidirectional relationship. Negative mood creates negative thoughts and negative thoughts create a negative mood. Likewise, positive mood creates positive thoughts and positive thoughts create a positive mood.

Positive or negative thoughts are not inherently helpful or unhelpful. They do, however, influence your thinking. Some types of negative thoughts that come from negative states, like fear or anxiety, are limiting. One of the challenging things about anxious thoughts is that they are noisy and take up a lot of internal space, trumping other kinds of thoughts. The very nature of anxious thoughts, left unchecked, perpetuates more anxious thoughts. As Charlie Brown famously stated, "My anxieties have anxieties."

Anxiety shows itself in a variety of ways, both physically and cognitively. One way it commonly shows up in thought is in the form of rumination. Ruminative thinking is like a hamster on a wheel; thoughts running feverishly without getting anywhere. When ruminating, it is common to replay the minutiae of something that makes us uncomfortable and this causes more discomfort. The more discomfort, the more we cling to familiar but ineffective means to address the discomfort (by thinking more) and the cycle continues. In addition to not working well as a strategy, the transient sense of control that this type of thought might bring comes at a high cost.

Overthinking Can Be Confused with Skillful Reflection

Olivia first came to therapy after taking a new position that she believed was a smart career move. But she had mixed feelings about the company culture. Her questions about the new position took the form of rapidly cycling thoughts that left her exhausted. She wasn't able to quiet the thoughts. They only got worse and tipped over to disruptive rumination which interfered with her sleep and was beginning to impact her ability to cope in general. She felt out of control. The chronic cycling of anxious thoughts was tipping over into depression. The ruminative thinking impaired her ability to skillfully address the real challenges at work.

In therapy, Olivia began to practice watching the content and nature of her thoughts. This practice helped her see how her thoughts became more rapid when she was uncertain and trying to gain a sense of control. She did this by thinking about all possible outcomes of future scenarios. Olivia would imagine herself responding to all imagined situations, practicing what she would say or what she would do. She came to see how this kind of thinking made her feel ill at ease and did not actually bring her a sense of preparedness or control. It exhausted her, interfered with her thinking, and made it more difficult to make decisions and take action.

How did Olivia identify when her thinking had tipped over into unhelpful thinking? She began paying attention to the rapidity of her thoughts. In the room with me, she listened to the sound of her voice and noticed when it became monotone and her speech more rapid. Until now, she had a belief that talking it out would bring relief but she recognized that this was not true when in the grip of cycling thought. I asked her to reflect on her experience of me when gripped by ruminative thoughts. When she was immersed in anxious thought she had less awareness of my presence. At these times, it was difficult to be aware of anything outside her thoughts.

Cuing into her present experience, the physical room, as well as her physical sensations, helped Olivia get a dispassionate distance from her unhelpful thoughts. Once her thoughts quieted down, Olivia was then able to focus on her experience of doubt and of feeling overwhelmed. Gradually, by witnessing the nature of her thoughts, she was able to step back from them and get a broader perspective.

Olivia gained clarity on the unhelpful nature of ruminating thoughts. Her thinking became clearer and she was able to successfully navigate her work challenges. Therapy gave her the tools to reengage with skillful reflection when she found herself ruminating. Olivia did not give up her thinking style of imagining different scenarios and her response to them. But now, she understood the difference between skillful reflection and overthinking.

Whether or not you have experienced high levels of anxiety, you probably can identify with overthinking. Overthinking is a misguided strategy of our minds, sometimes fueled by an incorrect belief that more thought equals greater understanding. Like Olivia, many of us overthink to prepare for all contingencies. Or maybe we have an untested belief that doing anything, including thinking, is better than non-doing in the face of discomfort. Or, often, there is no underlying belief but something our mind does automatically in response to uncertainty.

Naming Thoughts: An Important Step in Skillful Reflection

A helpful way to observe your thoughts is to practice naming them. Notice the specific thoughts and label them in some way. This helps you to both quiet your thoughts and set parameters around them. By naming thoughts, you will have a sense of how busy your thinking is. When are you more likely to overthink, overanalyze, or get lost in thought? What kind of thinking do you enjoy? When do you feel as if your thoughts are controlling you? What is happening within you when you find your thinking helpful thoughts? Unhelpful thoughts? What do you say to yourself that you might not even be aware of? When are you thinking in ways that promote flexible thought? Deeper thought?

As you practice noticing and naming thoughts, don't judge them or immediately try to change them. What is most important is to become an observer of the quality and quantity of your thoughts. Try to gain understanding as to how different contexts, especially your different internal states, impact your thinking.

Here is a list that I generated while reflecting for twenty minutes on my own types of thoughts.
1) the naming thought as I notice what comes into my awareness from my senses;
2) the associative thought to almost everything that comes into my awareness;

3) the attribution thought that arises from discomfort that has no actual relation to the source of my discomfort;

4) the pleasurable and expansive thought that comes from deep engagement with ideas and finding connections between them;

5) the reminder that I have to remember something thought;

6) the background words and half-sentence incessant thoughts;

7) the associative thought to noticing a physical sensation, like hunger and thinking about my next meal;

8) the thoughts that float through my mind right after I wake up that give me feedback about what I've been grappling with (give more space to these thoughts);

9) the repetitive list-making thought;

10) a getting ahead of myself thought about a future task as I'm engaging in the task at hand;

11) the narrative attributional thought about someone else's behavior that can't, in fact, be known.

Notice that this list has many unnecessary as well as a number of unhelpful thoughts! Developing intentional reflection is an ongoing practice.

I then generated a list of types of thoughts that I found to be helpful.

1) the naming thought as I notice what comes into my awareness from my senses;

2) reflecting upon what is right about me and my life thoughts;

3) intentional thoughts that consciously choose what to reflect upon;

4) the thoughts that float through my mind right after I wake up that give me feedback about what I've been grappling with (also on the prior list);

5) noticing that I've drifted from the present moment and gently bringing myself back thought;

6) the open and spacious thought that reflects on what others are telling me without cutting them off with my own narrative;

7) noticing and naming when I have an unhelpful negative response thought;

8) giving other people the benefit of the doubt under ambiguous circumstances thought;
9) thinking about a kind way to say something difficult to someone thought; and
10) reflective thoughts about how to integrate an intentional practice into my day.

The first item in both lists, the naming thought of what comes through all the senses, is a helpful way to stay present. Notice the lack of correlation between other items in the lists. Again, what is most important is increasing the number of helpful thoughts and quieting down unhelpful or unnecessary thoughts.

Be curious about the types of thoughts you have, and after reflecting upon them, make your own list. Practice this same exercise while in different moods. Generate names for the type of thoughts you have. Borrow my language in the prior exercise or make up your own. Identify which thoughts are helpful, unhelpful, and neither helpful or unhelpful. Notice how much time you spend in each. Notice their quality. For example, are they gently unfolding, fast and intense, looping and repetitive, curious?

The practice of skillful reflection is to patiently observe your types of thoughts without getting lost in them. Developing the ability to reflect upon your types of thoughts will help you become a more skilled thinker. With practice, your thinking becomes more deliberate. You can rely on it as a trusted, albeit imperfect, advisor.

Carve Out Time for Direct Reflection

Wise investigation (or direct reflection) on the five foundations of intentional living is a powerful tool that will eventually transform your thinking. Directly reflecting upon what is coming to you from all of your senses grounds your thoughts in your body. Wise investigation of what naturally interests you deepens your understanding and helps you stay perpetually curious. Other topics for direct reflection include the timeless, important questions—questions like "Who am I?" and "What is my purpose?" "How does my culture influence me?" "What are the greatest challenges facing us?" and "How do I best live in relation to these challenges?"

In this digital age, where your attention is pulled in so many directions, one of the costs is time and space for direct reflection. It is important to consciously carve out time for it. Reflecting directly on your experience, perhaps more than any other intentional practice, gives you a sense of being in the driver's seat of your own life. Direct reflection clarifies what gives you purpose and helps you focus your decisions and actions accordingly,

Chapter 7

Self-Talk in the Spirit
of Inquiry

The art and science of asking questions is the source of all knowledge.
Thomas Berger

I was fortunate to have had a wonderful mentor in my first professional job as a psychologist in a clinical academic research center. Keenly intelligent and worldly, Rachel had a wealth of professional wisdom to pass on. I learned much about being a professional by observing how she conducted herself in meetings and in front of larger audiences. I looked forward to our weekly one-on-one meetings, which focused on my administrative and clinical responsibilities in the center.

While Rachel was generous in her willingness to pass on knowledge beyond my immediate job responsibilities, my success in securing time with her was dependent upon my ability to keep her attention. To do this, she wanted to know, quickly, what my point was. I often didn't have a specific question or point because I was still learning to formulate the most relevant questions. However, if I didn't frame what I wanted to learn about in the form of a specific question, I would soon hear her kind, Parisian-inflected voice marking the end of our time together: "Are we finished?" or "My dear, what's your question?", a friendly but pointed reminder not to linger.

This was a formative experience. I internalized the importance of observation and how to ask the right questions. A good question holds attention and shines light on the most effective way to discover what is being sought. I often still ask myself, over two decades later, sometimes with a smile and a French accent, "My dear, what's your question?"

As a clinician, I am struck by how often clients ask me direct and heartfelt questions in a way they don't ask themselves. "How do I do this differently?" "Do I have to keep doing this over and over again?" "Why is this so difficult for me?" "What do I do the next time x or y or z happens?"

It makes sense to ask a trusted professional or teacher questions. At the same time, it is equally or more important to ask *yourself* what your heart and mind want and need to know. And—more important still—listen to your answers! Listen as if you have something of value to say. Even when you are confused or uncertain, your response to your own sincere inquiry provides valuable guidance. And you benefit most from the understanding that you, yourself, arrive at. You often know more than you give yourself credit for knowing. At the same time, you need to practice effective inquiry in order to access and develop your knowledge.

When exploring your mind ask yourself direct questions, rather than thinking about or inferring something. With direct questions, you are more likely to be clear about what can be known.

Even when not asking questions, we often try to make sense out of what is happening by making inferences that imply certain questions. Instead, practice asking yourself, "What, if anything, is my question?" and, "Can it be answered?" Then pause and wait for your response—yes, no, or maybe.

We don't always have to ask questions or know what the right questions are. Noticing without formulating a question is a great way to be present, observe, and learn. Yet practicing asking specific questions like, "What's my question?" and "Do I have a question?" trains your attention on helpful ways to make sense of experience.

Skillful questioning helps you perceive what is happening, both within and outside yourself, through an open lens. An open lens of attention is not layered with implicit questions, premature conclusions, and stories about your experience that unnecessarily limits it.

Learning to ask yourself pertinent questions, and listening thoughtfully to your responses, is a practice in reflection that takes time to develop. Consciously set out to become a skilled question-asker.

For skillful reflection, not only is the question important, so is the spirit in which you ask yourself the question. Directly ask yourself questions rather than thinking *about* them. Then, when you respond, pause again and take it in for a moment before rushing off into more thought. Don't ask your questions in a rhetorical way. Rhetorical questions don't take seriously the answer. An example of a rhetorical question might be, "Why do I keep doing the same thing over and over?!" or "How much longer can I can I continue to put up with this?" said with frustration but no real inquiry. Again, when you ask yourself a question to reflect upon, ask it sincerely and with curiosity. Care about your response.

Ask Simple Questions That Invite Direct Reflection

To practice skillful reflection, a good rule of thumb is to ask simple questions that allow for the greatest breadth of response. Two simple questions of enormous value are ,"What's happening right now?" and "How is this for me?"

By asking "What's happening right now?" and training your awareness on the question, you are inviting a pause and direct reflection. Your response can include anything—your sensory awareness, physical sensations, thoughts and half-formed thoughts, feelings, judgments, evaluations, ruminations. When you ask "What's happening right now?" in the spirit of sincere inquiry, you adopt a more dispassionate stance to witness the happenings of your mind. "What's happening right now?" shines the light on your mind's busy-ness and is a good start toward quieting it down.

When I train clinicians to work in an experience-near way with clients, i.e., a way that encourages the client's personal experience of an idea, I encourage them to use the question, "What's happening right now?", which is usually more helpful than the question "How are you feeling?" The challenge with "How are you feeling?" is that we don't always know how we feel. We might be more familiar with and habitually report one feeling over another. And feelings may not be the most relevant aspect of the experience. Paradoxically, the question "How are you feeling?" is more likely to bring you away from your body, which is the seat of feelings and emotions, into the realm of thought disconnected from feeling. In other words, "How are you feeling?" can take you away from the fuller breadth of your current experience. In contrast, "What's happening right now?" places your awareness on all aspects of experience, including your feelings.

Imagine sitting across from someone you care about who is talking about a painful experience and tears well up in his eyes. "I see your tears, what's happening?" indicates an openness that invites exploration of the sadness or any other feeling that is present. It also invites awareness of all other aspects of what is happening. He may have responded to happy memories of a loved one who died, "I remember how she played cards and made all of us laugh." Or, "I was thinking about what you just said and realized that I have never given myself credit before, always ready to judge myself. That makes me sad." Or the physical experience of what is happening may be most relevant, "As we were talking, I noticed this tightness in my throat, aware of the black ball of pain every time I think about the breakup, and wonder whether the pain will ever go away."

Don't limit the range of your inquiry with a limiting question. Helpful questions give you the greatest range of possibility in which to understand yourself and others. For example, if your loved one shared an experience of a black ball of pain, that is a powerful visceral experience. You can continue to be open and curious. Tell me more about that black ball. Is the black ball dense? Is it permeable? This kind of exploration of an image which came spontaneously from the interior, brought forth by a good question, gives insight into what is happening and, often, helps to let go of the painful experience.

My clients practice in this way outside of therapy sessions, throughout their day and in different situations. They practice pausing and asking themselves, "What is happening right now?" in moments of pleasure and discomfort, and in moments when they are not noticing anything in particular. Neutral moments, or moments that are not charged, allow you to notice more subtle sensations, thoughts, and feelings that can otherwise get overlooked or ignored.

The practice of asking "What's happening right now?" and other questions that are meant to place awareness inward can be misconstrued as being self-referential. It is a mistake to equate self-exploration and self-understanding with self-preoccupation. A capacity to consciously shine light on the workings of your mind—how you preference, take in, respond, react, and make sense of all that is happening within you—allows you to develop skillful reflection. This is why a practice in reflection is so important. It helps you understand the quality of your thinking, helps you move toward greater understanding of things as they are, and creates space for discovery.

A Good Question, "Is This True For Me?"

Another great question is, "Is this true for me?" It is important to understand what you are telling yourself and whether or not this is really accurate for you. The self-statements you make influence your experience and understanding. It is important that they not unnecessarily limit you.

In the room, when a client says something that is filled with energy, emotion, or conviction, we pause. I sometimes mirror back the content and energy and have the person reflect whether this is true for them.

Jennifer recently had an asthma attack while at work, the first in nearly a decade. Until now, her asthma had been well-controlled. The experience had shaken her up. In the room with me she animatedly described the experience of her asthma attack which created anxiety. "I was lying there on the floor telling people what was happening and I was freaking out! I couldn't handle it!" Jennifer now had substantial insight into her old belief that she couldn't handle a lot of things. In reality, she did cope with most things even when they were difficult. Now it was important to understand if this recent experience of the asthma attack and related anxiety had really left her feeling out of control and not able to cope.

I asked Jennifer to share more about her experience of not being able to handle what was happening. Her animated style shifted and she became quieter, slowing down and speaking more deliberately. In this slowed-down space she described the experience of herself while having the asthma attack as of being *both frightened and of being in control.* Her actual experience of the asthma attack was different than the story she told herself after the fact. Jennifer felt that she would be OK, her anxiety was not to the level of a panic attack, and she knew what to do to take care of herself. This experience of both being frightened and feeling that she would be OK was very different from her childhood experiences with chronic physical illness and not understanding what was happening. It was also different from her experience of just a year before when she had difficulty discerning the degree of her anxiety and when all anxiety was experienced as overwhelming.

Jennifer's capacity to pause and look at the fear of the recent asthma attack helped her discern the difference between being frightened and being unable to handle the situation. As a child, there was no difference. In her present circumstances, there was. This was an important recognition for her. Jennifer could see how physical correlates of fear triggered by something in the present evoked old beliefs of not being able to cope. She came to this transformative insight by pausing and asking, "What is happening right now?" and "Is this true for me?"

This recent frightening experience around illness provided an opportunity for Jennifer to reflect on the changes she has made and to further integrate them into her present experience. For Jennifer, "What's happening right now?" and "Is this true for me?" provided the chance to disentangle old connections and beliefs that were no longer true and didn't serve her. As a result of asking herself relevant questions about her most recent experience, Jennifer was able to have the insight that she had made qualitative changes in her characteristic way of responding to fear. She now saw that when old triggers arose, she had the capacity to view them from a new perspective, as an opportunity for further transformation of old, unhelpful beliefs. This type of meta-reflection is breakthrough thought that ushers in transformation in future thought.

Exercise: A Direct Way to Notice Experience

Find a place to sit quietly for five minutes. Close your eyes comfortably and ask yourself, "What's happening inside?" Try to witness for a few moments before putting words to what you are noticing. Then say to yourself what you notice as you notice it. For example, "I am thinking about what I'll make for lunch." "I feel tightness in my neck." "I feel restless." "Time is passing slowly." If what you notice is primarily your thoughts, try to direct your attention to your physical experience and continue.

Practice this same exercise for a couple of minutes at different times and while in different situations and internal states.

Good Questions Teach the Most from Experience

Karen, a young tech entrepreneur, recently sold her company to a much larger company, the holy grail of many young start-ups. Only three years earlier, she experienced tremendous disappointment, uncertainty, and fear when her first start-up folded. The company going under, after so much hope, sweat, and perseverance, shook Karen's confidence at its core. She had profound self-doubt and questioned her competence and judgment. She struggled with depression for a time during which she replayed in her mind, over and over, vignettes of meetings with potential funders that did not come to fruition and other possibilities that didn't quite materialize. Karen accumulated evidence of her inadequacies and built a case against herself.

Karen's self-indictment got in the way of earnest inquiry around what really happened and what, if anything, she could have done differently. (Sometimes it is helpful to wait before you extract lessons from experience. But since Karen was getting down on herself, it helped to test out the truth of her self-accusations.) Karen practiced pausing and saw that she was creating a story around what happened that probably wasn't accurate. The story came from a small place inside her, where she experienced the painful emotions of shame and embarrassment.

Now Karen started more consciously asking herself simple, helpful questions like "What is happening?" "What can be known now?" and, when she blamed herself, "Is this really true?" This kind of reflection enabled her to begin to answer herself in a dispassionate way, less skewed by self-doubt. Intellectually, Karen understood more than most people how in the area of tech, good ideas, experience, and hard work need a healthy dose of good fortune in terms of timing and financial support. Even so, it took time and practice in wise investigation to appreciate the skills she had brought to the company irrespective of the painful outcome.

Karen's shame and embarrassment lessened and she sought out trusted colleagues to help her explore the lessons to be gained from this experience. This process, while difficult at times, validated her perception that her ideas for the company were solid and had real potential. Karen was surprised and moved by how highly her colleagues regarded her. In the process of reaching out to them, she got multiple offers to join other companies. Karen took time to assess whether to stay in the tech start-up arena, given the intensity of the work and the long hours. She considered the conditions under which she would join another company or start her own.

Ultimately, she decided to start another company with her partner from the prior start-up. They added a third partner who was skilled at presenting big picture ideas to potential investors. They used the contacts they made in the first start-up, including investors who liked the initial idea but, for various reasons, were not ready to commit resources. Karen and her partners honed their message to several audiences early in the process in order to test interest in their product, which was directly related to the product developed by the defunct company. The new venture secured generous funding prior to a heavy investment of time and effort, a condition Karen had decided was essential in order to move forward with her own company.

Moving through depression and navigating a painful experience, Karen came out of it stronger and wiser. The demise of her initial start-up did not define her. She learned to differentiate unhelpful self-doubt from helpful self-questioning, the latter offering the real lessons. With time she got distance from the painful experience by asking relevant questions, pausing and reflecting, and then answering. For example, every time she told a story about her incompetence, she directly asked herself, "Is this really true?" She could now more clearly investigate past mistakes or gaps in knowledge without building a case against herself. Karen came to a more factually accurate and intuitively resonant understanding of what happened. She then used this information to forge the best path forward. This time around she was clearer, more seasoned, and better able to engage investors to support the new company.

Karen enjoyed the financial windfall from the sale of her company and she felt rewarded by the recognition and doors now open to her. Still, her greatest enjoyment comes from her belief in herself, and her knowledge that she has the capacity to be OK, more than OK, no matter what the outcome of her actions and endeavors. She was at a difficult crossroads and found in it an opportunity to discover new ways to practice embodying her values. Karen remembers her first start-up with tenderness and appreciation. She views that chapter in her life as having had provided her the seeds of growth that bore fruit three years later.

An intentional practice in asking helpful questions at the right time helps you become a clearer, deeper thinker. Asking these questions in the spirit of open inquiry enables you to more comfortably take risks that are in line with your aspirations.

Chapter 8

The Empty Search for the Whys of Discomfort

Obsessed by a fairy tale, we spend our lives searching for a magic door and a lost kingdom of peace.
Eugene O'Neill

Searching for reasons, for the *why* of our discomfort and conflict, is one of the single biggest misallocations of human effort. Searching for causality is a problematic leap that our brains often make. Correlative associations are the best we can accurately arrive at in most situations. Uncertainty is inherent in life and things happen which are often outside of our control. Yet most of us spend a tremendous amount of mental and emotional energy searching for clear causes that are inherently elusive and usually nonexistent.

Searching for causes that can't be known gives external circumstances too much power over your well-being.

Why *Why* is Often Not the Best Question

When used sparingly, consciously, and in a context where the question can deepen thought, *why* is a useful question. But the habits of the mind that search for reasons that cannot be known as a means of trying to get control over uncertainty is an empty sort of reflection.

Curiously, you are more motivated to pursue theories of *why* when an experience is unpleasant or you would like it to be other than it is. You are less likely to search for the *whys* when things are going smoothly and you are at ease. When things are going as you'd like, do you wonder why they are going well? Most of us do not. If searching for causality was driven by rationality, and the pursuit of *why* was helpful, it would be more productive to create theories of *why* around life situations that are going well or internal states that you want to perpetuate.

When you are uncertain, upset, or uncomfortable, your ability to observe what is happening is challenged. You are naturally motivated to end discomfort and pain so your mind has a tendency to turn away from the current experience. When this happens, you can jump off the *what* is happening to the imagined *why* of it. The switch to a not-helpful pursuit of *why* happens so quickly that the strategy of turning away from direct observation is not even noticed. The brain mixes up helpful reflection with unhelpful storytelling which impedes your ability to see things as they are. And, importantly, this causes you more discomfort and makes it difficult to move on. The brain's attempts to end discomfort keeps it alive!

Here is an example. Imagine being out of work and waiting to hear whether you get a second interview for a new job. The first interview went well and you are hopeful that you will be called in for the next round of interviews. You are told by human resources that they will contact applicants within a week or two. To remain calm and enjoy your week, you try not to think too much about it. On the morning of day seven, when you still haven't heard, your discomfort increases. Though you try not to dwell on it, little *whys* manage to encroach on your awareness. "Many people are on vacation this month." "This if often how it goes, these things always take longer." Soon the front line innocuous *whys* give way to more nervous-making *whys* as the uncertainty drags on. "The third person I interviewed with looked preoccupied. I wonder if her mind was already set on someone else." "Oh no, I bet they looked at my college grades (from over a decade ago) and saw the "C" I got in biology sophomore year! I knew that was going to be held against me." Or, "I shouldn't have so readily talked about my children. They might think I'm not really interested in my career."

Exercise: Shift from *Why* to *What*

Think of a time when you thought a lot about a situation and you conjured up stories, or *whys*. It might be helpful to choose a situation where you were disappointed or upset at the outcome and it was difficult to let go. For example, you didn't get an opportunity that you wanted or someone you cared about didn't return your feelings in the same way. Write one such situation down. It might help to choose one circumstance that you remember clearly but is not painfully present for you right now. Then write attributions or causes that sound like something you may have come up with at the time. Now, reflect upon the same incident with the question "What was happening?", staying only on what could be known. (e.g., "My confidence took a real hit." or "I just couldn't understand it.")

How can you move from unhelpful thinking to fruitful reflection? First comes Awareness. Learn to notice the way your mind tells stories as it is happening. Easier said than done. These kinds of stories are in the form of *thinking about*— thinking, thinking, thinking. Once you recognize that you are scanning and searching for causes that cannot be known, you are in a position to reflect differently, in a way that will become helpful to you in these situations. This is a great place to be, but it is not a comfortable place. At these moments, it might not be helpful to give yourself a directive like, "just sit with it." If it were easy to sit with it, you wouldn't be so uncomfortable in the first place.

One way I create space for myself in moments of discomfort is to remind myself how little control I have over most things. When I initially say this to clients they often look at me strangely. Once I, myself, recognized how frequently my mind searched for ways to grasp control over what I had no control over, I could finally begin to lay down my burden. What a relief!

Your brain doesn't, deep down, believe that your made-up stories are reality and that is one reason why thoughts keep cycling around and around. Once you recognize how little control you have over most things in life, you are better able to assume responsibility for the often neglected areas where you really do have control. This is incredibly liberating. The very act of direct reflection on what can be known is doing just that: shaping your thoughts and, ultimately, your life.

Letting go of all attempts to exert mind-control over what can't be controlled, you are now skilled at quieting your mind from chasing its tail. You become more curious about what can be known and bring clear-eyed and helpful reflection to it.

Focus Your Reflection on What Can Be Known

For wise investigation, a good place to start is to notice and verbalize only what can be known right now. "I am hopeful and excited." "Excitement is tipping over into doubt!" "She didn't respond in the way I had hoped." "I feel gratitude." "I feel rejected." "I am taking a risk with these unknowns."

Paradoxically, stating the overlooked obvious is often the most challenging.

Naming what is happening right now can bring comfort because you are speaking a truth that you do know. You don't have to search for deeper reasons. "Can I make room for this pain without forcing myself to stay here?" "Can I recognize that I feel overly responsible for others without needing to take action on it, which is my habit?" "What, if anything, can help me get out of this rabbit hole of self-doubt?" These kinds of questions allow for a middle ground between running from the experience and harsh directives to stick it out, neither of which are helpful. Your ability to skillfully reflect is aided by gentle and persistent encouragement to find ways to be more at ease with what is happening right now.

With practice and skillful reflection, discomfort with uncertainty is lessened because it is not layered with your struggle against it and attempts to avoid it. Trusting that you will be OK, no matter what, nurtures a willingness to stay engaged with what is happening without jumping to theories of *why*—theories you probably don't actually believe.

It is not realistic to set a goal of stopping the unhelpful pursuit of *why*. You cannot stop your brain from doing what it does automatically. Instead, try to notice when you have moved away from the experience and are now searching for causes. Notice the first moment when the thought arises (e.g., "If I were more x, y, z he would have asked me out on another date.") Can you bring yourself back at these times, not for the purpose of submerging yourself in bad feelings, but to gain trust in your ability to create space for all experience? (e.g., "We seemed to get on so well and then he stopped calling. That is so discouraging.") The shift from storytelling to skillful reflection has the potential to free you from personalizing painful experiences.

When you slow down and first begin noticing what your mind does with discomfort, you can become impatient that there is nothing to be done about the experience. A common feeling or response is something like, "OK, I'm not jumping off to distraction (or self-repercussion or whatever). Now what?!" Continue to notice and see what happens, and also, bring a spirit of gentleness and compassion to the experience. When I first offer this suggestion to clients I sometimes get puzzled looks or a response akin to, "Is that the best thing you have to offer me?" When clients are struggling, therapists too can be tempted to jump in with interpretations that are a version of a theory of *why*, which ultimately is not helpful.

Keep pausing and noticing. Notice when the discomfort is less acute.

Notice when you feel something other than discomfort. Notice what happens when you catch yourself asking *why*. Notice what happens when you bring yourself back to what is happening now. You might ask yourself, "Is there something that might help me in this moment?" Place your awareness on the fruits of this practice, even if they don't initially seem bountiful. This helps you gradually build your capacity to pause before automatically creating unsubstantiated stories; laying the groundwork for more helpful, direct reflection.

With time these very moments that are uncomfortable or painful become opportunities to transform your life. These experiences are your best teachers. This is not cliché. Learning how to allow what is happening without making up *why* stories helps you move through the discomfort better because you are not adding struggle to what is already challenging. This initially seems counterintuitive—just like getting a bad cramp in your foot and being told to walk on it. Actively accepting when *why* can't be known, you become much clearer about the *what* of your experience. This is the path to actually discovering more about the *why*s.

By staying on your direct experience of what can be known, there is no need to look for some *deeper* cause of your experience. The path to deeper exploration is direct inquiry of what is before you in the present moment.

Understanding Why Comes From Reflecting on the What

Jordan walked into my office visibly upset at how angry he had gotten at his five-year-old son, Thomas, during one of his son's meltdowns. After several unsuccessful attempts to defuse his son's escalating upset, he grabbed Thomas roughly by the wrist and brought him to his room for a time-out. Jordan was still shaken the following day when I saw him. He felt it was important to understand more about what happened that led to this degree of anger.

Jordan began to explore familiar themes of struggle with which he was very familiar. He spoke of his differences with his wife in parenting styles and how he didn't always feel aligned with her. He spoke about his relationship with his father, and how his father's judgmental style he now, at times, saw in himself. While these explorations were valid, they were primarily intellectual and were not accessing the visceral experience that had left Jordan shaken. As he continued, his felt experience with Thomas was becoming dimmed in the exploration of it now. If we continued down this path, an opportunity of gaining deeper understanding would be missed.

I asked Jordan if he thought it might be helpful to take a few minutes in hypnosis (a way of pausing) and invite yesterday's experience with Thomas here now. He was familiar with working with me in hypnosis to deepen experience and he readily agreed. I invited Jordan to revisit the experience of Thomas's temper tantrum. I asked him to talk to me about what he was experiencing while in this state.

Jordan began recounting his impatience with Thomas. While recalling it in the room with me, there still were no palpable physical or emotional correlates to the anger that Jordan believed left him shaken. There was no evidence in the present moment that he had had a level of anger that was experienced as out of control, or that was out of the ordinary for a parent who was exhausted from being tested. It could have been that the anger was so unacceptable that Jordan was now cut off from it. But my experience of him up until now was that he had the ability to access difficult emotions, including anger.

Because something clearly was upsetting Jordan, and anger was not present experientially in the room earlier or in trance now, I invited him to explore the physical sensations happening in his body right then. He quickly noticed a tingling in his neck. I asked if we could move away from the exploration of anger, letting him know we would return later if it was helpful. I asked him to stay with the experience of the tingling which was physical and immediate. Often visceral experiences are a guide, leading to images, memories, and important insights.

No images arose for Jordan around the tingling so I asked him if he could simply stay here and welcome whatever arose next. I asked that we keep hanging out with how the experience unfolded without asking anything more of it. This gave Jordan permission to stay in this relaxed state without needing to intellectually understand what was happening. Spending time in this open way, for as little as a minute or less, without trying to think his way out of an uncomfortable state, can lead to a deeper understanding. This was an invitation to expend no effort—and allow the physical sensations to lead the way.

The tingling in Jordan's neck gave way to a pervasive and powerful physical experience of being filled up. This sensation spread from the center of his chest out across and down into his stomach. Now Jordan welled up with tears and identified the physical sensation as being love, love for his son. He experienced this degree of love as overwhelming and wondered out loud whether he had ever loved like this before. Alongside this powerful experience of love, Jordan also had an awareness of tremendous fear of losing Thomas. He quietly cried as he stayed present to this newfound awareness of how vulnerable he felt in relation to his son and to this experience of deep love. He had an emotional awareness that if he lost his son his life would never be the same.

Jordan had never felt this vulnerable before. His son's out of control behavior, and Jordan's inability to soothe Thomas or set helpful limits with him, led to Jordan's awareness of how little control he had over others, including his son. By staying with the *what* (and here the *whats* were physical sensations), rather than the *why*, Jordan felt a sense that led to a profound awareness of his core vulnerability around deeply loving another person.

This vulnerability around deep love is the truth for all of us if we allow our hearts to open fully. The more we love, the more there is to lose. Allowing this vulnerability is the only way to be authentic and live fully. Jordan's experience of powerful vulnerability in the face of love, not his anger, was what had shaken him. This insight came to him when he paused and stepped away from *thinking about* what happened; when he stopped looking for the *whys* of his experience.

An unexpected outcome of this exploration was that Jordan continued at times to physically feel a tingling in his neck. This became a reminder that he could hold onto. It helped Jordan when he was exasperated with Thomas. It also helped him approach his wife differently, with more compassion, when he was upset and felt she wasn't supporting his parenting efforts.

This tingling, the memory of the experience, gave Jordan a sense of expansiveness. It gave him hope that he could make different choices when handling difficult emotional situations. Importantly, by paying attention to the physical experience, Jordan had a memory that could not have been conjured up by the rational, analytical mind. Future tingling was evocative of the awareness of his vulnerability in allowing himself to be so touched by his love for his son. This is a great example of how focusing on what is happening right now—and making more room for all your experience—allows for deep understanding that your problem-solving brain cannot envision.

A lovely follow-up occurred several months after this session. Jordan found himself stressed and irritable on a weekend away with his wife and son. Noticing this, his son asked him if he'd like to take a time-out to help him feel better. Jordan, deeply moved, took his son's advice and spent time in his workshop, which was a special place for him. He also asked his son to join him in this place where he usually spent time alone to recharge himself. The hour they spent together will be a lasting memory for Jordan—and maybe for Thomas, too.

Part III

Choosing

Chapter 9

How to Make
Better Decisions

Liberty, taking the word in its concrete sense,
consists in the ability to choose.
Simone Weil

Every day you make countless choices as part of the routine management of your life. You pay bills, practice self-care, clean your home, shop, make social plans, return emails, and plan for your future. In your relationships, you negotiate who does what in the day-to-day management of living. If you have the financial means to have others help manage life's details, you have relationships with them around how these things get done.

In modern life, you have more choice than ever before. Does so much choice put you in a better position to skillfully make decisions? Do more options create a sense of greater volition? Probably not. Having too many options can actually hamper good decision-making. Generally, the more options available, the more psychic energy it takes to choose, and the less satisfying decision-making becomes.

Many decisions are made entirely outside of conscious awareness. Even when conscious, we aren't so good at identifying what actually influences our decision-making. As more choices are available, we are less likely to consciously make decisions. Because we are inundated with advertising and so much choice, now—maybe more than ever— it is essential to become a more intentional decision-maker. Conscious choosing requires that we learn to tune out options that are distractions.

Psychologists Daniel Kahneman and Amos Tversky conducted groundbreaking research in the way that decisions are made and found that we are often biased and irrational. One common decision-making bias is the default bias. When people have a high cognitive load, or a lot going on, they choose the status quo or what is familiar. Since our lives are more hectic and distracting than ever, this isn't promising for making intentional decisions. Choosing what is familiar is a fine choice if consciously chosen. However, returning to the status quo by default is often an avoidance of practicing intentional choice.

Bring Greater Awareness to the Act of Choosing

Choose to choose. If you fall back on the familiar, make it a conscious decision. Choosing to choose means accepting the responsibility of making decisions that help you take meaningful action toward your aspirations and in alignment with your values.

Making wise decisions requires two things: consciously reducing the amount of choice to be made and, importantly, practicing intentional choosing.

Your current choices shape your future choices. The decisions that will likely shape your life for the better require active engagement and sometimes tough choices. Be an active participant in the decisions that shape your life. Give thought to what decisions are worthy of your time and effort. Establish practices to help you arrive at decisions that reflect what is most meaningful.

Anne, a young creative and aspiring urban designer, often came to sessions looking like she just woke up. She was nearly paralyzed by an inability to make decisions. Anne wanted to move beyond semi-interesting part-time jobs toward developing a name for herself in her profession but was unclear how to move forward. She was unclear about many things.

Routine decisions threatened to overwhelm Anne. For example, while sitting with her morning coffee she thought about whether to drop off laundry on the way to work or wait until her day off. If she dropped it off on the way to work, should she also go to the food co-op? She then had difficulty sequencing the two activities. Planning when and what to eat that day could also overwhelm her. How would she find the time to buy and prepare healthy meals? Every consideration was a complication that morphed into a sticky ball of confusion.

Because she often felt overwhelmed, Anne typically avoided making decisions until she could no longer put them off. As a result, she was in a constant state of catch-up and disorganization. Her indecisiveness made her feel badly about herself. In addition to chronic anxiety she was becoming depressed, which worsened her existing organizational challenges as well as the cycle of fear around making decisions.

I asked Anne to create a list of a dozen or so decisions she encountered on a typical day, without giving it much thought. Then, take the list and create a hierarchy in terms of their importance as well as their urgency. Anne returned the following week with a diagram with dozens of items listed. In addition to the main list in the center, there were many items scrawled in the margins. Looking at this pictorial representation of her thought process, I had a felt understanding of Anne's experience of confusion. For example, there was no distinction of whether changing her cat's brand of food was more important or immediate than taking steps to pursue a new job.

At this point I wondered if, in addition to psychotherapy, Anne needed cognitive remediation. It turned out to be unnecessary. By placing her awareness on the inner turmoil and confusion that arose during the act of choosing, Anne got some relief from the pressure to choose. With less pressure, she was able to select just one or two decisions to focus upon. With less fear and pain in approaching making decisions she could more effectively explore her relationship to choice.

With practice narrowing her focus, Anne got snippets of clarity about her preferences and priorities. Importantly, she recognized how difficult it was for her to emotionally let go of any possibility because of painful self-doubt. She believed there was a right choice and didn't trust herself to make it. By shifting the focus to her self-doubt and fear of closing doors, Anne saw that she did have preferences but had little faith in her ability to effectively pursue them. As Anne continued to take small steps in making decisions, she gradually felt able to test out and own her decisions. She felt empowered to recognize her budding clarity on what she wanted from work, from herself, and from relationships. Knowing her priorities, she could now take meaningful steps toward them.

You likely aren't incapacitated by everyday decisions. But what would it be like for you to create a hierarchical representation of your choices? Do you know which decisions are most central and timely in relation to what you find most meaningful? Do you spend too much time engaged in activities you did not consciously choose? Do you feel as if the obligations of your current lifestyle leave little room to choose differently or to change course? These are important questions to explore.

Exercise: Create a Decision-Making Hierarchy

This exercise will help you reflect upon where you place your time and energy in decisions now, and what changes could be made to better align them with your core values and aspirations.

On one piece of paper, make a list of the decisions you have made in the past week. It might help to first write down on a separate piece of paper all that you can think of. Include both mundane choices as well as more complex decisions, like those related to longer-term goals. Include choices that you want to make even if you have not yet made them. Then take the list and rank them in order of importance. Put the decisions that are related to your core values and long-term goals on top. If you are not clear, that's OK. The purpose of the exercise is to help get clarity.

Reflect upon the hierarchy you have created. Ask yourself questions in relation to this decision-making tree. Which decisions, if any, are challenging for you? Which are easy? Which are you delaying or avoiding? Which aren't important but still urgent? Which ones could you do away with? Which decisions matter to you but aren't related to your core values? Do any of these choices seem big and weighty? If so, what is your approach to them? Toward which of these decisions do you think you are more intentional? Where do you think you can make inroads into being more intentional?

Simplify the Decisions You Need to Make

Your time and energy are important assets. They are finite. Don't waste them.

Shape your life by simplifying your decisions. Consciously reduce the number of choices you make. Save your resources for navigating decisions that will make a lasting impact. Hone your decision-making skills on choices that will enrich you. Routinize aspects of your day by consciously making choices in advance. Doing so helps declutter the day-to-day management of your life.

Routinize decisions by becoming a minimalist most of the time. For example, consciously choose in advance what you wear and eat during the work week, how and when you exercise, and what you do for other forms of self-care. This way, you can better prioritize making other choices, especially challenging ones, while still implementing prior choices around healthy living. Enjoy spontaneity and new experiences when you have the time, energy, and quality of presence to appreciate them!

A few years back I simplified my clothing choices, making more careful decisions in what I bought, kept, and wore. This required time and thought up-front but ultimately ended up saving a tremendous amount of time. Before this I didn't always exercise conscious choice in buying clothes. I shopped haphazardly, picking up what appealed to me without consideration of how it functioned in my life. I didn't know all that I had and some of my clothes went unworn. This didn't align with my value of living simply.

Practicing more conscious decision-making in buying clothing has saved time in thinking about what to wear and time spent in stores. Shopping less, I feel less pulled by material things. Now when I buy clothes, they generally need to meet the criteria of comfort, quality, style that reflects me, and generally fits in with what I already have. I still occasionally spontaneously shop and buy things that are outside my typical style, especially when I travel abroad. But now when I do, I make sure to wear it. As a result of more intentionally choosing my clothes, I now like them more and think about them less.

To reduce the number of decisions you need to make throughout your day, it can be helpful to begin your day with a one-minute reflection on what choices, if any, you want to focus on that day. Be specific if you can. Of course, unexpected and urgent things may come up that need attention. But having clarity approaching your day helps you stay on track. A less cluttered mind helps you to be more responsive to whatever arises that needs your attention, and to set limits around it.

To practice intentional decision-making, simplify your life in ways other than routinizing decisions. Live within your means and have a healthy relationship with money. Debt that doesn't grow in value or add to your life in meaningful ways decreases your long-term freedom to choose.

Are you more attracted to things than experiences? Notice if a lot of energy is directed toward bright, shiny objects which detract from choices that enrich your life. Bright shiny objects are anything that is compelling but, ultimately, empty because they don't enrich you. They might be the latest technology apps, fashion trends, ideas, or people du jour. If you find yourself distracted by shiny objects, it may be because you have difficulty making and enacting decisions that add to your sense of yourself as authentic and your life as purposeful. Shiny objects shine even brighter when you experience self-doubt or uncertainty. Focus within, not outside yourself, to prioritize your choices.

Let your decisions reflect what is most important to you. Decide for yourself what you need to bring into your life. If your choices leave you unfulfilled, re-evaluate them. Be willing to get rid of things that clutter your mind, and life, and unnecessarily commit your time and resources.

Become a Student of How You Actually Make Decisions

How we think we make decisions and how decisions are actually made are often very different. For example, emotion plays a large, often underestimated and misunderstood, role in decision-making. The bad news is that decision-making is often biased and irrational. The good news is, as individuals, we can become students of our own biases. This will make us better decision-makers. Behavioral scientists and neurobiologists have documented a relatively long list of tendencies that get in the way of making effective decisions. This knowledge can empower us to do things differently.

Making decisions that align with your core values requires thinking outside the box as well as being open to challenging your current views. Cognitive biases, though they help you make decisions more efficiently, also thwart your capacity to think broadly and flexibly. For example, in addition to the status quo bias (preference for the familiar) mentioned earlier, we tend to agree with people who agree with us. We are better at seeing the error in another person's thinking than our own. We prefer pleasant experiences in the present and avoid the pain or difficult things for later. And, when we make a bad decision, we try to rationalize it rather than learn from it. As you can imagine, these biases aren't particularly helpful for complex decisions that require flexible and creative thinking.

At the same time, you can overcome bias through practicing intentional choice. You have the capacity to reflect on your relationship to making decisions: how you formulate them, implement them, and evaluate them. Become aware of what kind of decision-maker you are. Consciously making decisions is the best strategy for implementing effective action.

For years I had a style of comfortably following my intuition. When the decisions were weightier, either because they involved a large investment or mattered greatly to me, I generally took time to explore options and weigh them. Sometimes I overweighed them; afraid to choose. Probably my most difficult situations were when I had to find someone to partner with in implementing my decisions. An example of this was when I interviewed general contractors around a construction project. One of my biases (unfortunately unrecognized for a long time) was that when I enjoyed an interaction with someone, I would be less likely to gather the kind of information needed to make the best decision. This happened, at times, because I did not have enough information on hand. But more often it happened either because I got caught up in an enthusiastic conversation, or because of an unexplored belief that a good connection to the person meant she or he was the best person for the job. This bias, or underlying belief, impaired my capacity to evaluate who was best for the job beyond the initial connection.

Fortunately, this bias did not lead to catastrophic results. Sometimes it worked out well. But too often the process became more fraught then it needed to be. Once I practiced more intentional decision-making and became more skilled at identifying my own bias, I could be clearer on how to approach decisions that would lead to more effective work partnerships. Of course, connection remains an important consideration to me on projects that involve an ongoing relationship. But an over reliance on a good first impression no longer interferes with my ability to ask important questions that help me arrive at the best choice.

How do you make decisions? Like most of us, you probably have ideas of how you make decisions that don't jibe with reality. And, like most of us, you probably are more effective choosing in some areas and less effective in others.

Paul, a young aspiring writer, came to New York City to find a writing community and develop his writing voice. One of his gifts as a writer was his attention to detail. Paul let writing develop organically without editing himself prematurely. He trusted his intuition and also sought feedback when he felt his work was far enough along to show others.

Paul's writing style was in stark contrast to his interpersonal style. In social situations, he was filled with self-doubt and anxiety. Each conversation was weighty; every interaction was make or break. He overthought social interactions, believing there was a *right* and a *wrong* choice of what to say and how to behave. Unlike when writing, socially he constantly edited himself and imagined others were judging him. Paul's painful self-judgment and overthinking, fueled by his biases, effectively shut down his capacity to be spontaneous in front of others.

In therapy, Paul explored how he made decisions in different areas of his life. His ability to allow thoughts to flow unimpeded while writing helped him feel creative and confident. What got in the way of allowing this same freedom in social situations? Framed in this way, Paul examined an underlying core belief that he was uninteresting; that he was unformed in terms of his identity. He believed everyone else had more conviction in their beliefs and more clarity about who they were. This comparison to others made him feel lonely and inadequate.

Paul hadn't before considered the possibility that others his age also grappled with questions around identity, and that those struggles could actually make you interesting. Paul had an untested and inaccurate notion that he had to know with clarity who he was and what he believed in order to be interesting. Testing out these assumptions helped him to take more risks socially. He became more spontaneous. His conversations became more interesting because he wasn't judging every word that came out of his mouth. Paul also stopped putting pressure on himself to craft wonderful conversations. When a conversation wasn't particularly engaging, he didn't automatically retreat to his old belief that it was do-or-die and reflected poorly on him.

Can't Choose Clearly When in a Stuck Place

Belinda was a lawyer in a competitive law firm where a sixty-plus hour work week was common. She came to therapy because of constant anxiety around how her performance was evaluated at work. Because of a near-exclusive focus on billable hours, Belinda feared she wouldn't make her hours when she got assigned a new type of case and needed to take time to learn. Instead of recognizing that learning curves are a given, she felt inadequate. Belinda felt conflicted about taking earned and much-needed vacation. She felt guilty around being caught "sneaking out" at 7:30 p.m. to come to therapy. This unhealthy environment was negatively impacting how she felt about work and her well-being in general. Yet, she couldn't perceive better options.

In therapy Belinda focused on the emotional toll of the past two years at this job. She enjoyed working hard, but she also wanted a rich life outside of work. As a result of work-related stress, she experienced less vibrancy in her important relationships. Belinda came to understand that she had choice if she was willing to exercise it. "What's becoming clear from this past year in this law firm is that I don't want to be in an environment where I feel as if

I am being assessed in a crazy way ... or where the determinants of success are disturbing to me." However, she still didn't perceive available alternatives that appealed to her.

Belinda began exploring in-house options where the work was competitive but without the constant grind of documenting hours. Until now, she had avoided exploring in-house options because of a belief that doing so would take her out of the running for more prestigious positions. She was programmed to view in-house jobs as safer and saner, but less challenging and less highly regarded.

Belinda's current unhappiness was contributing to a limited either/or view of possibility. Either she had a more intentional and gratifying work/life option *or* a respected job in her profession. I encouraged her to get clarity on the qualities of work she valued, including in her current job. Could she use these preferences as a guide? Could she be open to types of work that she did not yet know about? Could she let go of stories that kept her stuck and unable to imagine alternatives? I also asked that she think about how to live more simply in order not to place her salary above all other factors in considering what her options were.

Sometimes we can cling too tightly to a dollar amount and limit other ways that abundance, including financial abundance, can come to us. Choosing intentionally requires a willingness to let go of things that may be attractive but don't add to life in substantive ways. When you enjoy work *and* it allows space for other things you most value, you end up engaging more fully at work You may even get more recognition at work because you are inspired.

Belinda did find another job and did go in-house. She waited until she found an organization with a culture that matched her values. She took a job with a company that challenged her and valued team dynamics. Belinda still occasionally works on weekends but, far from expected, it is appreciated and not taken for granted. She no longer needs to account for every hour of her day. She is rewarded for what she brings to the company. For example, her new position values and utilizes her fluency with multiple languages, something that she had not experienced in the old firm. Far from being the *safe* bet, Belinda feels challenged daily. Her earlier cognitive bias of in-house positions led to an avoidance of fully exploring her options. Belinda's awareness of her decision-making bias helped her test out what was actually true for her. Testing out her inaccurate underlying belief helped her find a job that enriched all aspects of her life.

Exercise: Examine Your Decision-Making Skills

Reflect on the following questions related to how you make decisions. Think of specific examples for each question.

- Do you rely on snap, intuitive judgment when you make decisions? If so, in which areas?
- When do you think quick, intuitive decision-making serves you? When has it led to error?
- Are you a deliberate, even cautious, decision-maker? If so, how does this style work for you? Has deliberateness tipped over into avoidance?
- Which decisions are you most likely to avoid?
- Do you have difficulty, or even get overwhelmed, making decisions? If so, in which areas?
- In which areas do you trust your decision-making skills?
- When do you doubt your decisions?
- What is one complex decision that you are facing? How do you approach it? How might you more skillfully approach it?
- How can you implement more intentional choosing in your daily life? Think of one thing you can try out in the coming week.

An Intentional Life Clarifies Best Options

When you experience yourself as authentic and living with purpose, endless options are not a distraction or a pull. What is more important to you is that you perceive options relative to your value-inspired goals, and that you trust your ability to create options and make important decisions.

Practice bringing increasing awareness to how you make decisions. Be curious about when and where you are vulnerable to bias. Evaluate and learn from the decisions you make. Reflect upon the outcome of your decisions and how you feel about decisions after the fact. Prioritize those decisions that are in line with your core values and aspirations. Live simply, routinizing decisions that are a necessary part of everyday life. Don't accumulate material things or experiences that require energy to sustain but don't add meaningfully to your life. Be willing to take risks in your decision-making for the sake of what is of central importance to you. Choose wisely around what you wish to bring into your life.

Chapter 10

Allow for Possibility That Is Not Here Now.

My mother's menu consisted of two choices: Take it or leave it.
Buddy Hackett

Mark, fresh out of completing a master's degree in business, was hopeful about work opportunities. Before returning for his MBA, he had worked in the art community. He wanted to utilize his new degree in that field. Mark made the decision to go back to school because there was a scarcity of job opportunities within it. He believed that the few positions that opened up went to people with years of experience, good connections, or who had their own money to fund projects.

Applying for jobs post-degree, Mark was deflated to discover that the opportunities available to him now were nearly identical to the ones available before. The positions that could utilize his skills, and where he could earn a living, were still few and far between and seemingly impossible to obtain. He felt like he was back at square one, except now he was saddled with a huge amount of debt.

Mark gave himself four months to find a position within his chosen field.

When he was still without work after four months, he felt he needed to expand his job search. Mark initially viewed widening his search as a personal failure and had difficulty summoning sincere interest. Yet he also believed that actually working was more important to getting himself back on track than what the job was. He was concerned that the longer he was out of work, the less employable he'd become.

Mark initially went through the motions of sending his resume out. When he read his cover letters, his own words rang hollow. He was feeling lost in the process but still continued to show up for it. In therapy Mark explored the deflation he felt while, at the same time, tried to gain access to confidence in himself. He wanted to make room for real possibility, even as he was currently unable to envision it.

Mark knew that faith in himself was important in order for others to believe in him. On the first couple of job interviews he had difficulty presenting his best self. Knowing his struggle was not serving him well, he tried to bring more openness to future interviews. Even if he didn't think he wanted the position, could he stay open to the person interviewing him and to the company? Mark tried to approach each interview as if he had a choice though he didn't believe it at times. This was an important but difficult balancing act.

Mark stepped back from the impulse to immediately try to sell himself as the person for the job and instead brought curiosity about the company and the position. He asked sincere questions about the company, its employees and its mission. As a result of his shift in stance, of his willingness to be open to new options, Mark surprised himself and enjoyed the interviews. He felt his confidence returning. He still experienced fear at times because he was low on money and had little structure in his day-to-day life. Yet he was coming to believe that it would be OK and that he would find work.

Most importantly, as Mark practiced allowing for greater possibility than he initially envisioned, he became interested in some of the positions for which he was interviewing.

Mark then interviewed with two companies related to the arts which were looking to fill traditional business positions. While he had envisioned himself in a more creative position, with his new sense of openness he now saw this kind of opportunity as uniquely suited to his skills and training. He became enthusiastic about one of the companies, a tech start-up with a mission of introducing the arts and working artists to a larger audience. The hiring team returned his enthusiasm.

Mark wouldn't have known about this company and this position had he held onto his earlier, narrower perception of his preferences. His willingness to expand the field of possible options brought him to this place that he couldn't have earlier imagined.

There Is Possibility Beyond What the Mind Inhabits

To widen the field of choice, two practices are helpful. The first, is to have clarity on your current preferences. What would you like to see happen as a result of the decisions you make? The other practice is to broaden the scope of imagined options, allowing room for unimagined possibilities. This second practice requires having an awareness of the inevitable limitations of your current view of what is possible. These two practices in tandem allow for the clearest and most flexible decision-making.

Mark's ability to emotionally make room for options outside of his initial job search required that he examine his approach and understand what was limiting his ability to move beyond his initial disappointment. This exploration led to an awareness that he was not only disappointed about the lack of opportunities, but that he also devalued other options. He mixed up preferences with value judgments. Because of this, he judged all options that were not his preference as inferior. And he judged himself as lacking because he could not get the kind of job he preferred. No wonder he couldn't bring authentic interest to his expanded job search.

In widening your options, it's OK to have preferences. You should! Know them well. Your preferences are a good starting point in your decision-making process. At the same time, your preferences are limited to your current understanding of what is possible. Can you know and respect

your preferences and, at the same time, eliminate limiting check lists?

Preferences are based upon a number of things, among them past experience, judgments, values, internal state, and memories. They are important to respect but also know that they can narrow the imagination. In understanding your preferences, and the meaning you assign to them, you have the ability to change how you make meaning. When you don't label preferences as "good" or "better" and as simply "my preference," that is an important step in expanding the scope of options. Knowing preferences, divested from value judgments, frees you up to make decisions more flexibly. And the more flexible you are, the more you open yourself to seeing the potential in a greater range of options.

Divesting preferences of value judgments has another important benefit: you are less likely to view yourself as lacking if you are not chosen. It is freeing to accept your preferences without judgment, and to also feel good about yourself when you are not someone else's preference.

Allowing for greater possibility includes recognizing that external circumstances place parameters around your options. But these external parameters are often not as limiting as the mind's limitations.

How do you make room for possibility that you can't yet imagine? How can see yourself as having options that you don't really believe in the moment? You sincerely *allow* for the possibility of having additional options, even when you can't perceive them in the present. Otherwise, you will approach decision-making with a yoke around your neck. You recognize the limited view of what you are able to imagine right now at this moment. Recognizing this, you have the ability to create new options by expanding your imagination. You may need to exercise choice within the options that you perceive are here for you right now. And you may need to learn what is necessary to lay the foundations for other options. What matters, under these conditions, is the spirit in which you make your decision. Choosing the best option, even under less than ideal circumstances, is an important step in creating better future options.

You also have a choice regarding how you perceive yourself as a decision-maker. Do you view yourself from a compromised one-down position, that when your preferred option is not available you have to settle? That "beggars can't be choosers?" This view limits your ability to build on and learn from the decisions you have already made. This *settling* kind of thought comes from a fearful, limiting state of mind and ensures that you will feel compromised no matter what decision you make.

If you approach any decision as an examination of which option is the best one under conditions as you currently understand them, and allow for possibility that you cannot see at this moment, you are honing your decision-making skills. Instead of feeling limited by current external circumstances, you can be interested in the challenges that lie within them. Instead of being limited by your preferences, you can challenge them, finding the opportunity that lie beyond the current parameters of your imagination.

As you make and implement decisions, evaluate them along the way by asking the question, "How is this for me?" This kind of open question provides a framework to hone your future decision-making skills. It frames the question in a way that shines the light on your ability to be a more conscious participant in the decision-making process.

When approaching making a decision, notice your relationship to what is not available at the moment. For example, do you feel discouraged and perceive the roadblocks more readily than the opportunity? Alternately, do you perceive options that are not realistic under the current circumstances? Do you limit alternate possibility because you can't immediately imagine how to get there? Do you devalue options other than the one you want? Are you curious and open to them? Are you afraid to choose because you don't want to close off other possibility? Are you clinging to a possibility that's not here right now? Do you feel as if you are capable of generating further opportunity? If so, what are ways that you can do this? How you answer these questions will give you important insights into your relationship to choice.

Fear is the Greatest Limitation to Choice

Fear impedes your capacity to make intentional decisions, especially when you are making decisions in ambiguous circumstances. Fear prevents you from seeing all options and clouds your ability to envision incremental steps toward goals. Fear makes the "why I can't" more pronounced than the "how I can." And fear makes you doubt your capacity to make good decisions.

When decisions are made from a place of fear, you simply can't open to your options and make the most of them. You will approach making decisions in a way that, even when something works out well, the outcome cannot be fully appreciated.

When fear is present, you are more likely to avoid making a decision. Avoidance is an enemy to wise decision-making. When fearful, there is a strong preference to choose the safest or most familiar option in order to avoid whatever seems threatening. Consciously avoiding a threat might be a wise decision. But avoiding decision-making because it feels uncomfortable or threatening impairs your ability to be a good decision-maker. Avoiding as a habit makes it difficult to distinguish what is a real threat from what is an imagined threat.

When you are afraid you are less likely to examine all the relevant variables that will help you make the best decision. Why? Because fear shuts down curiosity. Fear narrows your attention as you try to avoid any anticipated negative future outcomes. All meaningful change involves risk so avoidance as a strategy deprives you of the substantial benefits of conscious risk-taking.

Humans have the same physical circuitry for fear as non-human animals. However, the human conscious experience of fear (as far as we know) is different. Cognitively, we are less likely to worry about physical and imminent danger as we are about something that might turn out badly.

Fear appears in different guises. Sometimes we clearly recognize what we fear. But more often than not our fears morph into other concerns and take on disguised forms.

Three particular types of fears affect your ability to be a good decision-maker: The fear of becoming overwhelmed in the face of events beyond your control; the fear of not being good enough or worthy (a close relative of this fear is the fear of mediocrity); and the fear of not having enough or of losing what you have.

The fear of being overwhelmed or unable to protect yourself against unanticipated events can lead to a preoccupation with trying to get control over things which are beyond your control. When this happens, you might spend more time trying to avoid a bad outcome than making decisions that will lead to life-enhancing change. This might show itself as a fear of risk-taking. Or, paradoxically, you might take unwise risk by making compromised choices that are likely to turn out bad, which then confirms the perception of needing to protect yourself from risk-taking. If the fear of being unable to take care of yourself holds sway, it undermines your ability to take charge of what you do have control over, which is your response to the outcome of your decisions.

The second kind of fear, that of not being enough and its offshoot, fear of mediocrity, is fueled by two pervasive habits of mind. The first is *comparison mind* which is the unfortunate habit of viewing yourself relative to other people. The other related habit is *being judgmental*. Feeling both *better than* and *less than* others, both inferior and superior, are two sides of the same coin. Either way, you are making choices from a small and disadvantaged place. Comparing yourself to others is different from looking to others for inspiration. Comparison mind diminishes a healthy sense of self and leaves you feeling separate from others. For example, you might believe that other people don't struggle as much, or know more clearly what they want to do, or are able to find love more easily than you. Even when comparisons are objective, they don't lead to effective movement toward your best self. Comparison mind leaves you feeling disconnected and isolated.

Being judgmental interferes with feeling free to experiment. When you are judgmental, whether self or other-directed, you feel a need to justify or prove yourself. Perfectionism, a relative of the judging mind, chokes creativity. Self-criticism doesn't motivate you to do better. Just as children don't learn how to do things in new ways by telling them what is wrong about them, the same is true for us as adults. When you aspire to change, free of judgment of yourself or others, then the choices you have are not as emotionally-laden and limited to a preexisting bar that you need to live up to—a bar that is impossible to reach.

The third fear that impairs decision-making is the fear of not having enough or of losing what you have. This fear can lead to holding tight to what you have because you don't trust that the future holds abundance. It leads to a distorted view of what you need. Money becomes overvalued rather than playing a healthy supportive role to what is actually most important. The fear of not having enough is pronounced in a consumptive culture that reveres wealth for wealth's sake and admires rich people over creative and generous people. In order to transcend limiting beliefs, it is important to understand how your culture influences, and limits, your choices.

The fear of not having enough also inhibits generosity because giving to others can feel like you are giving too much away. The fear of deprivation can lead to keeping a tally of investment in relationships rather than giving freely in them. It interferes with the ability to develop mutual and generous relationships with others.

Right now, you are enough and you have enough. Make decisions like you believe this to be true.

Hostage to Fear of a Disastrous Outcome

Jonathon visited his parents in London at least twice a year. His parents were divorced. Jonathon was grappling with whether to make a quick trip to visit his father for his 70th birthday without contacting his mother. His relationship with his mother was fraught and had been for years. His two siblings had cut off ties with her. His mother was angry at him every time they spoke by phone because he didn't call as often as she would like. Jonathon, who had begun practicing intentional choosing, came to understand that his decisions in relation to his mother were strongly influenced by a deep fear that something would happen to her. And now, he feared he would carry the weight of guilt for not visiting her on this trip. Jonathon had difficulty making a decision because he could not discern chosen obligation from guilt. As a result, he was resentful of his mother and dreading the trip entirely. He didn't feel free to celebrate his father's birthday without seeing his mother. He believed he would experience remorse if he chose the trip he really wanted.

Placing awareness on how he approached choice helped Jonathon see that he was hostage to fear. He had experienced fear that something would happen to his mother ever since he was a small child.

Now practicing intentional choice, Jonathon was clear that he didn't want to visit his mother on this trip and that it was OK not to see her. He wanted special time with his father. He now could emotionally distinguish between chosen obligation and guilt. He recognized that if something were to happen to his mother, it didn't happen *because* he chose not to visit her on this trip. Jonathon let go of the niggling thought that allowing himself time with his father unencumbered by a visit to his mother was selfish. By allowing himself the option of taking the trip in the way he wanted, he was able to feel compassion for his mother and her way of suffering that pushed everyone away from her. Feeling free to choose, Jonathon was more able to be present to his mother in a way that didn't feel overwhelming to him. He freely chose to have more frequent phone contact with her.

Befriending Fears Helps You Make Better Decisions

If your choices are overly influenced by fear and efforts to avoid fear, then your decisions cannot add to your life in substantive ways. Choices driven to alleviate fear—of being overwhelmed, unworthy, or not having enough—are mostly unconscious. Even when the choice made from an intentional practice is identical, the consequences of a choice based on fear enriches you less. Practicing intentional decision-making addresses fear directly, offering the possibility of making wise choices even in the presence of fear.

Can you treat your fears that limit you as if they are misguided children? If a frightened child is acting out, do you shame him? Do you let her avoid what she is afraid of, when doing so gets in the way of her development? These aren't effective strategies. The best solution is some version of showing love and making room for the fear, while helping the child soothe herself and navigate her fears. The same applies to your own adult fears.

Don't berate yourself for your fears. Don't judge them. Respect them and be open to them. At the same time, don't allow them to rule the roost. Treat your fears with compassion while setting limits around them. Understand them without giving them free reign. Learn how your fears influence how you make decisions. How do you protect yourself? How do you best take risks?

Knowing your fears intimately, without giving into them, allows you to test out whether they are really true. If they are true, does it have to be that way? And if the fear is your reality, can it become less limiting for you? Softening around your fears enables you to be see choices more clearly, and feel more comfortable around choices that you make.

Only by befriending your fears can you make wise and effective choices. How do you begin to do this? By practicing fearlessness.

Fear naturally arises because you have the capacity to reflect upon the human condition and all its uncertainty. But by practicing fearlessness you come to trust your ability to cope with all outcomes, to learn from them, and to make future decisions increasingly in line with what matters most and your core values.

Fearlessness is possible when you accept that you are good enough and you are lovable enough, right now, regardless of your flaws and regardless of how things turn out. Fearlessness is not the absence of fear but, rather, a quality of courage where you open up to what you fear. It is a practice. To be fearless, listen more to yourself and less to external messages about what will make you worthy, happy, and loved. Fearlessness lets you—slowly and patiently—let go of the need to defend. You defend less because you now trust your ability to protect yourself and make wise decisions that serve your interests.

Implement Decisions in the Face of Uncertainty

"If you can dream it, you can do it" is Walt Disney's famous adage. For many of us there is a perceived paradox in how to realize our dreams. On the one hand, the clearer and more vivid we can conceptualize dreams, the clearer the steps we can take to realize them. Vagueness is not our friend, specificity is. On the other hand, our dreams are developing as they unfold. They change as we move toward them.

Without making choices in relation to your dreams, they remain in the realm of fantasy. Practice choosing concrete steps, and implementing them, in order to evaluate how to keep moving in purposeful directions.

Dreams evolve as you create them. You evolve along with your dreams. It is a two-way relationship. Your dreams cannot evolve without making intentional choices.

Choose to focus on decisions that have the greatest chance of enriching your life. Be willing to take risks in the service of your core values. Don't limit yourself to the options you can envision in this moment. Learn what you need in order to create desired options. Be aware of your preferences without being bound to them. Become aware of what you fear and how your fear limits your ability to make bold decisions.

By learning to meaningfully expand your range of options, while understanding current external givens, the best way forward for embodying your most authentic life will become clearer over time. This doesn't mean you will have certainty regarding what decisions to make. It doesn't mean that your daily reality will neatly line up with your dreams. But you will trust your decision-making more, trust your capacity to choose well, and shape your decisions in a way that enables you to move toward what you value most, regardless of the outcome of any particular decision or action.

Part IV

Acting

Chapter 11

Wise Effort is the Best Kind of Action

Dreams pass into the reality of action. From the actions stems the dream again; and this interdependence produces the highest form of living.
Anaïs Nin

How do you take action in ways that create the kind of life and world that you want to see? How do you act in alignment with your own interests and in collaboration with others? By practicing intention in action, your actions best reflect your core values and make you an effective actor. Acting is a dynamic verb. While an action takes place in a circumscribed period of time, the practice of acting is fluid and continuous. It extends in time from before the action is taken to well beyond the visible results of the action. Bring your awareness to the entire continuum—doing so will positively influence the way you approach and take action.

How to Act with Greater Intention

To practice intentional acting, it is important to understand the difference between *acting* and *doing* because they are often conflated. When there is no distinction between acting and doing, unnecessary or misguided action is sometimes taken, often with a very different effect than we intended.

You cannot control how the external world responds to your actions, but you can take ownership of the spirit in which you act.

Action is most effectively taken in response to a conscious choice. What percentage of your actions is intentional? 5 percent? 10 percent? 20 percent? These may sound like low numbers, but think how much of the time your actions are automated and unintentional. How much of the time do you engage in distracting, time-passing actions that are not clearly chosen? Automated actions aren't a problem as you perform the mundane tasks of your life. Yet it benefits you to bring greater awareness to these tasks as well. Without a practice in intentional acting, a high percentage of life slips into going through the motions. When this happens, your experience of being a meaningful actor in your own life is diminished.

In order to act with intention, it helps to distinguish intentional action as distinct from doing. In many people's minds, they are one and the same. Here, doing is defined as action that is not conscious. We are programmed *to do*, to be busy, to take action regardless of whether it is even needed. Both intentional action and doing require expenditures of time and energy. Lack of discernment between the two results in chronic doing, which interferes with your ability to effectively shape your life.

Chronic doing is what happens when you have difficulty pausing and being still.

By practicing intentional action, the proportion of time and energy spent in conscious and deliberate action increases, and the proportion of non-mindful doing decreases. With continued practice, non-mindful doing is no longer a default position and your actions become more focused and effective.

Wise Effort Understands When and How to Act

Wise effort is the whole-hearted commitment to consciously direct your energy towards what matters most to you. It is a cornerstone of living an intentional life. Wise effort asks the question, "What, if anything, can be done now?"

If effort broadly represents how you direct your energy, what is action in relation to effort? Wise effort is not synonymous with action. It is the ability to know when to act with intention as well as when inaction is the best option. Wise effort clarifies when action effectively serves your goals and values. Through wise effort, your actions are aligned with your values and they shape a life of purpose regardless of the outcome of any one particular action. Wise effort helps guide your thoughts and choices in a way that allows your actions to be responsive and flexible rather than reactive and inflexible.

Wise effort includes both intentional action and restraint from action, and non-doing.

Sometimes wise effort requires restraint from action. This is true both when you are reactive and when you determine that the time is not ripe for meaningful action. Understanding effort as related to, but distinct from, action is important because it helps you discern between refraining from action and disengaging from what is happening. Refraining from action is a conscious and intentional act. Disengaging from what is happening is inactive and leads to non-intentional acting. It is not wise effort to adopt a nihilistic stance, (e.g. "Why bother?"). Avoidance of taking action is not a strategy of wise effort.

It is easy to think of times when we have been reactive and it would have been better to hold off from taking action. For example, when someone said or did something that hurt us and the only thing that came to mind was to say or do something that hurt the other person in return. We may have tried to cloak harmful comments in elaborate language and justifications but the end result was not helpful. At the moments where the only way you can act is to react, wise effort requires that you refrain from action. When you practice wise effort, you don't experience this restraint as inhibiting your voice but, rather, as choosing to rest in your real strength.

Non-doing, here, means an engaged restraint from action or effort. It is a form of stillness and quiet, a special kind of pausing. Non-doing is not inaction nor is it disengagement, zoning out, becoming distracted, or wasting time. Because non-doing is foreign to many, it can feel inactive. This is because we can have limited perceptions of engagement (i.e., engagement only as productivity) or moving toward a goal. Cultivating non-doing is an important skill that creates internal spaciousness. The actions that arise from this place are enacted with greater ease and clarity.

There is a concept in Taoism called *wu wei* which describes a paradox of "action without action" or "effortless doing." It is a natural state of non-striving that is cultivated. In this state, you let go and stop trying to achieve. It is not that you don't set goals or take purposeful action, but you try to cultivate a state in which you take yourself out of the central role of your life, in order to more fully understand the nature of things around you. You understand not by quickly trying to make sense out of things or by placing your stamp on them, but by simply taking them in.

So, what does non-doing look like in daily life? How do you begin to create an intentional practice of non-doing?

A non-doing practice starts by incorporating stillness and quiet into your day. The activity itself is not so important, though some activities lend themselves to non-striving more than others. It helps to identify activities that quiet you down rather than ramping you up, where you are engaged yet relaxed. What is important is the spirit of the undertaking. Can you set aside time in which there is nowhere to be, and nothing that you have to do? This is the spirit of non-doing, of *wu wei*.

Generate one or two such actions for yourself. Carve out small blocks of time, starting now, every week. In the beginning it is helpful to schedule it. Non-striving can be one of the most difficult things to make time for. Here are some possible exercises in non-doing: drawing, strolling, meditation, listening to music, meandering, slowly preparing a meal, gazing with gentle attention. It is helpful to be away from your phone. Though some people may make the argument that listening to guided relaxation or meditation apps are a helpful form of non-doing, if your phone pulls for your attention, put it away.

As you create space and time for the spirit of effortless doing, you are heightening your awareness of noticing times when you act mindlessly, or without intention.

I personally like to take walks without any thought of where they will take me. I try to commit to one daily walk, even if only for ten minutes, where I am not trying to get somewhere. I try to walk without getting lost in thought, which is a continuous practice. While in a state of non-doing, I constantly discover things. The same street, even if I have walked it dozens of times, reveals something new. I try to notice with all of my senses. I notice what it feels like to walk in all seasons, in weather I like and weather that is difficult to go out in. Now it is more challenging to practice non-striving as I walk because I have established a goal of walking at least 10,000 steps a day, which creates striving. Still, while intentionally engaging in non-doing, I do not look at my step counter as I am walking. Adding a goal to walking, even if healthy, makes me appreciate how easily I tip over into striving!

A wonderful non-doing practice is meditating in the morning for twenty to thirty minutes. Other non-doing practices that work for me are weed-whacking or ironing clothes while listening to a classical playlist composed of slower movements. I approach these activities with the intention to engage in what I'm doing without letting my mind wander someplace else. I practice these activities as a meditation. Yes, on some level there is a goal (eliminating weeds). But using an inexpensive weed-whacker doesn't make a dent on a four-acre plot of land. The point of all these activities is to quiet down my mind and cultivate non-striving. Done in the spirit of *wu wei*, these activities create feelings of peace and well-being. These non-doing practices also help quiet my mind at other times. They encourage me to bring more deliberateness to my actions when I am moving at a faster pace or acting in a goal-oriented way.

⁓

Wise effort enables you to have clarity on when and how to act, to feel confident in taking action, and to feel good about it regardless of the immediate results of your action. When you feel free to act, and the impetus for action comes out of a clear awareness of your priorities, the results of your actions don't matter as much. You trust that you will keep taking conscious and deliberate action which will eventually bear fruit.

What Kind of Actor Are You?

Most of us have uneven skills as actors—better able to pursue goals in some areas than in others. For example, some people act in ways that promote well-being in their personal lives but have difficulty doing so at work. Other people have rich friendships but find it difficult to take meaningful action to meet someone for a potential romantic relationship or partnership. You too may feel that you can make the most of opportunities in some areas of your life but not in others. Maybe in some areas you easily take steps toward your goals and in others you can't even imagine where to begin. You may be confident as an actor in some areas, and insecure in others.

Every one of us benefits from bringing greater awareness to the way we take action. Bring curiosity to your own style. Doing so will help you experience yourself as the central actor in your life—which is key to experiencing yourself as authentic.

As you place greater awareness on your style of acting, here are some questions to ask yourself: "What kind of actor am I?" "How do I take action: boldly, tentatively, somewhere in between?" "When am I more likely to be thoughtful and deliberate when I act?" "When do I act in a way that is mindless?" "How have I changed as an actor in the past five years?"

Sometimes desired outcomes, as well as disappointing outcomes, change the way we approach taking action. Can you think of an outcome that made you bolder, or more timid?

How do you approach taking action? Do you think about your options at length? Do you go over and over possible outcomes before taking action? Do you act quickly and evaluate after the fact? When would your approach to taking an action benefit from more reflection? When would it benefit from less thinking? How does your approach to taking action change when you perceive greater risk? How does it change when you are really invested in an outcome?

Can you commit a full month to studying your approach to taking action, and to finding ways you can be more intentional in how you approach and take action? Notice when your actions are intentional and when they are not. Which actions can you take without intention because they are routine? Do you consciously make them routine or are they default actions that weren't chosen?

~

Historically, I had a style of habitually underestimating how much I did. As a result, I had an inaccurate perception of my actual free time. I would become enthusiastic about a project and make decisions based on my expansive internal state without thinking through the implications for shaping my future time and resources. I loved immersing myself in projects and learning new things. But as I've gotten older I have chosen to be more discerning around which projects are most likely to align my interests and values. This has helped me to feel more purposeful. It's OK to get fired up with enthusiasm, but I don't always need to act on it. Or I can act on it in smaller, circumscribed ways. Over time, I've learned to hone my enthusiasm so that I am more likely to get fired up over projects that jibe with my core values. Importantly, I have also learned to enjoy life when there are no projects.

An example of how I practiced intentional action was when I took stock after putting a bid on a small, easy-to-maintain bungalow in a bucolic town in the Catskill Mountains. I did this to have year-round access to a larger plot of land which is a haven that restores and inspires me. My time there is spent walking, reading, and simply gazing—in solitude and with loved ones. On the land, there is a non-winterized studio barn and a vintage airstream with breathtaking mountain and valley views. But it is difficult to share with guests because it has no running water.

I did not build a house on the land because I wanted it to be a place where I enjoyed nature and nothing else—no house projects and no thinking about what's next. (Though I did spend countless hours designing a house with the help of an architect—only to go with converting the existing barn.) Buying the bungalow helped me combine my desire to spend more time on the land, including in the winter, as well as provide a suitable place for friends and family to stay.

After my bid on the bungalow was accepted my first response was joy. That joy was quickly coupled with apprehension and doubt. "Would I really be able to maintain the place with little effort?" "Would I lean into creating projects in the house that distracted me from ways I preferred to consciously expend my focus and energy?" "Would I feel free to not visit the house should I want to spend time traveling elsewhere?" And even, "Will I regret this?"

This fear was a response to a recognition of my old style of jumping into projects that were enriching but also complicated my life. Inevitably, there was the question, "Am I being impulsive?" When doubt is present it is easy to question whether decisive action is actually impulsivity. In this instance, the fear provided an opportunity for further reflection on the spirit in which I had taken action.

Through direct reflection I saw that the fear was real but likely unfounded. I moved forward because it was possible to have a relationship with this house in a way that honored my wish to live simply and also share my land with others. If I was wrong, I did not have to have a long-term relationship with the house. So far, it has been low maintenance and served the purpose I had hoped it would. I did fire up early on and committed time and resources to renovate it, but did not get caught up in countless design details as I would have in the past. Now, when I find myself imagining new projects for the house (because my mind still loves to create projects), I stop myself. I ask myself directly, "Do I really want to do this?" And the answer generally is "No."

Time Out from Habitual Action Leads to Creative Solutions

Joanne came to therapy in the midst of overwhelming anxiety. Her business was having fluctuations in revenue at the same time that she was implementing costly plans for its expansion. Joanne owned a company that required that she constantly generate new product lines which were produced all over the world. To keep things running smoothly, she traveled frequently. When home, she often woke up in the middle of the night to speak with manufacturing contacts across the world and in different time zones.

Being entrepreneurial in her line of business nearly assured that Joanne lived with constant stress and uncertainty. Anxiety was familiar to her but its intensity and chronicity was now exacting a painful toll. She recently began seriously questioning the sanity of her lifestyle. Joanne had my name and number for some time, but when she initially heard that I worked with mindfulness, it sounded foreign and counter to knowing herself in a rational way. She kept my number anyway and called when her level of anxiety reached unbearable levels and she was willing to try anything.

Joanne dedicated herself to the therapeutic process in the same way she approached everything: all in. At the time she called me, she also began exercising most days. Therapy and exercise were important pauses for her and ones that, until recently, she could not have imagined making time for. The very act of allowing herself time for self-care was a major shift and therapeutic in and of itself.

Therapy was a place where Joanne dared to question how she was living. This took courage, and she feared her explorations could lead to dropping the ball on her responsibilities. It was new for her to pause and examine her values and desires without quickly jumping into action to immediately address every challenge. A nagging question at the back of Joanne's mind was whether she would want to walk away from her current lifestyle.

Joanne's anxiety quickly lowered to much more manageable levels, but her discomfort did not. She had the insight that she valued a certain amount of baseline anxiety because it motivated her. This insight led to an important exploration of Joanne's beliefs about what made her successful, and how her answers were at odds with feeling ease and spontaneity. Joanne learned to pause and ask herself how she experienced things as they were happening. Pausing, without acting, initially led to a sense of feeling lost that she didn't like. Still, Joanne persisted and practiced tolerating discomfort without acting. On some level, she intuited that this was an important practice for her.

Eventually, her experience shifted from feeling lost in a way that was not OK to feeling lost in a way that was OK, and maybe even beneficial. What felt like "lost" was actually not acting in a driven way, which was Joanne's habitual way of moving toward her goals. This *lost but OK* feeling was an experience of non-striving, which alternated between feeling aimless and having the experience that something important was happening. Joanne came to understand that stepping back from habitual action was uncomfortable but not passive—far from it. Yes, she was stepping back from her business activities in some ways. But, because of it, she was coming to notice new possibilities. Internally Joanne was moving toward a major shift in how she conducted business.

In her newfound capacity to pause, Joanne was making room for changes that she considered in the past, but they had seemed like distant possibilities. Acting with greater intention provided the framework to make bold decisions. Joanne began to allow others in the company to step up more, and even requested that they do so. She focused her awareness on ways of taking action to support staff in their efforts to solve challenges and problems more autonomously. She provided guidance which initially required greater effort on her part. It was important that the people around her understood the implications of Joanne's internal shifts in terms of what it meant for their job responsibilities. She accepted that some changes in personnel roles were needed and practiced kind and direct ways to deliver difficult information to employees who resisted the shifts that were happening.

For some time, it remained a challenge for Joanne to step back from her identity as the main problem-solver. Stepping back from action was not inaction, but instead a radical shift in how she approached and expended her efforts within the company that she built.

She gradually shifted from a stance of addressing a crisis, which was the experience of out-of-control anxiety, to one of radically shifting how she acted in her life. This is wise effort. Joanne fundamentally transformed her drive to act. She still feels the urge to jump into action without pausing. But now she notices it and has greater choice in how to act (or not act).

Joanne learned to identify different ways of directing her efforts that led to radical change. First, she developed the capacity to pause before acting. Joanne now understood that action that is not driven, or reactive, leads to greater ease and well-being. She took a leap of faith and practiced letting go of striving, and saw that she could still work hard and act on her behalf. She now understood that non-striving was not the same as disengaging, and in some ways took greater effort. Joanne's commitment to learn to act with greater intention opened up new opportunities for her in business. Most importantly, by becoming an intentional actor she made room for a new, freer way of acting in the world.

How to Proactively Act, Rather Than React

When you react rather than proactively act, the outcome of your action comes at an emotional cost, even if you get the results you wanted. When you are reactive, there is an urgent sense that action must be taken immediately. You are more likely to lash out. Sometimes acting out of a place of reactivity gives temporary relief but ultimately make you feel worse. Examples of actions that arise from reactive states are: unskillfully confronting someone; trying to be right; or overpowering someone else in words or actions.

Wise action requires the opposite of reactivity. It demands restraint. Sometimes action is urgently needed but most of the time it is not. It only feels that way. Most of the time, stepping back and creating more internal space—stepping back from reactivity—is what is most urgently needed. Pausing from reactivity prepares you for those infrequent times that urgent action is required.

Reactivity is often caused by negative emotions, but not always. Anger and related emotions such as resentment, chronic annoyance, anxiety, and irritation create the internal conditions that prime us to be reactive. Emotions like fear and shame can lead to reactivity because they make us feel small and lead to responding from a one-down position. Anticipating difficult interactions can also prime us to respond reactively. Negative emotions are not inherently problematic. But if we don't have practice in working with them, it can be difficult to skillfully respond to them.

Stress of all kinds can lead to reactivity, and hectic lives leave little internal room to respond with equanimity. It is important to create the conditions that minimize unnecessary stressors. Positive events can also cause stress as we try to make room for them. We see this with children who sometimes have emotionally challenging moments after a long, exciting day. They can have difficulty regulating that much excitement and it can turn to irritability and tears. The same applies for adults when stretched to their limits. When we have chronically busy schedules, even if filled with things that we enjoy and value, it is difficult to practice wise effort. To live intentionally, we need to take meaningful action that will obviate the negative impact of stress in our lives.

Painful and traumatic experiences from the past can also prime us to be reactive in certain situations. Our bodies respond with cellular memories of the pain or trauma that are lightning-fast and intransigent. Under these circumstances, we might need help practicing non-reactivity when our bodies respond to stressors from the past, even if the present circumstances are different. The practice of moving toward less reactivity under these circumstances can be painfully slow and we need to be patient and compassionate with ourselves. Our bodies can continue to trigger us for a long time.

We cannot quickly change our bodies' response to being triggered. What can change under these circumstances is our response after being triggered. Intentional practices can mediate our corresponding actions to triggers so that they become more skillful and less reactive. Over time, our internal response can also begin to change as we break the external cycle of reactive action.

An intentional life is not devoid of reactivity. It is, instead, a commitment to understand the conditions that make you reactive. With understanding, you practice pausing as a way to create internal space and dispassionate distance from the reactivity, so that you don't act out of the unhelpful urgency of this state. An important way to do this is by bringing compassion to yourself when you are in the midst of feeling reactive.

An internal experience of reactivity is not inherently problematic. Sometimes the experience of reactivity has something important to tell you. Maybe you haven't been paying attention to your feelings or some external situation that needs your attention. Don't judge or dismiss the experience of reactivity. But also don't be controlled by it. You generally have more options than perceived while in the urgency of this state. Remember that your ability to act with intention is hampered when feeling reactive. If you react, rather than act with intention, the outcomes—even if positive—don't enrich you as they would if you had acted from a proactive, grounded place.

―――

When Liam turned fifty, he was pleasantly surprised to feel deep happiness when he reflected upon how he now experienced himself and his life. He felt content, was clear on his priorities, and had worked hard to make time for them. For the past two years, Liam had practiced intentional action in order to enjoy his life more. And, then, a few months after his birthday, it was as if the contentment had vanished. As was his style, Liam had taken on more projects than he could sustain in a healthy way. His levels of stress, which made him irritable, were now interfering with his close relationships and his enjoyment of life.

Liam generated a list of all his activities that required a time commitment. His practices in intentional action up until now did not include actually listing his activities and how much time he gave to them. Liam knew he was productive but was taken aback when he placed his awareness on the sheer number of activities. For example, outside of his job and family commitments, he had numerous roles in committees and on boards. While he valued these activities, he knew that something had to give. He knew that he would continue to repeat this pattern of reactivity if he did not take a new approach.

Liam chose a radical approach to free up commitments, including considering early retirement. Even thinking through on this possibility helped him see that, while he wasn't ready to retire, he wanted to continue working full-time only if he could transform his approach to his job. He had already taken small steps but recognized he now needed to take more definitive action. Liam spoke to a fellow senior partner and there was surprisingly little resistance. But it was up to Liam to implement the changes. He needed to turn over some of his day-to-day responsibilities to junior colleagues. Liam also met with colleagues in other organizations and let them know that he needed to make a substantive shift in his time commitments, even if it meant stepping away. He was touched to discover how he was valued and how colleagues took it upon themselves to create less taxing ways for Liam to stay involved.

Within a month, Liam returned to a state of contentment. Rather than perceiving his earlier reactivity as a problem, he now understood it as an important source of information. He used the experience of reactivity to deepen his commitment to act with intention and to take meaningful risks. For Liam, this meant challenging his style of taking on too much, and being willing to let go of activities. He received an overwhelmingly positive response from others. But this was not guaranteed. Liam's willingness to challenge his way of acting in the world, because it interfered with his well-being, transformed his experience of himself and created openness to options he had not before considered.

—————

If you can be a more intentional actor just 5 percent of the time, it will make a difference. This will set the foundation to act with greater intention 10 percent of the time, which is transformative. You will have greater clarity on how and when to act. If you are proactive rather than reactive, even when things aren't going how you would like, you will not find yourself in a state of waiting for things to get better. You will continue to take meaningful action in ways that serve your interests. You aren't invested in any particular outcome because you know that, regardless of the results of any particular action, you are empowered to act on your own behalf.

Chapter 12

Focus on the Effort, Not the Outcome

Satisfaction lies in the effort, not in the attainment;
full effort is full victory.
Mahatma Gandhi

All outcome is uncertain. We often resist this truth. When we do, we suffer.

Intentional action requires holding lightly to the wish that things will happen in a particular way. You've heard the dictum "it's the journey, not the destination." But letting go of a strong attachment to the results of our actions does not come naturally to most of us. It is easy to cling to wanting what we have worked hard to attain.

Holding lightly to outcome means that while you maintain a clear vision that guides your actions, you loosen the grip of desire on what happens as a result of the action. Focusing on the effort, not the result, is a skill that requires practice to develop. With practice, you'll act with greater flexibility, which then makes you a more effective actor.

A metaphor to help you act with intention is to think of your life like a long, meandering river. The path of the river is not a straight line--it changes as it meets rock and picks up sediment. The river's edges and water levels are in frequent flux. It grows larger as it collects water from tributaries and streams. Over time the river creates a wide valley so that it can flow unimpeded to meet the ocean, which is its destination. In an intentional life, think of your destination as becoming your most authentic version of yourself. Like the river, your life branches off in different directions as you make choices and take action. Your life course shifts in ways you can't predict or control as you encounter opportunities and challenges. While you know the general direction you are headed, it is folly to try to dictate the specific course beforehand. As you practice wise effort, your actions enable you to more effectively impact your life, paving the way to move with greater ease within a life that fully embodies what you value.

We Live in a Culture Obsessed With Winning

The frequent adages about staying present and enjoying the process are at odds with a cultural obsession with winning. There is pressure to accumulate accomplishments and be number one. This is so prevalent that we can conflate accomplishments that are the result of ongoing meaningful effort from those that are, for example, resume padding. A number of years ago, while working in a university research clinic, I occasionally hired research assistants. Most of the resumes I received were from young adults just out of college. I saw a number of five to ten page single-spaced resumes. Sure, they got bad advice on how to write a resume. But the bulky documents also reflected the excessive pressure to report long lists of accomplishments by the time they graduate college. There is pressure to be an expert before you have had the time to develop expertise.

Our cultural obsession with a winning outcome is nearly ubiquitous. Take for example the passionate frenzy over professional sports teams. There is nothing like an exciting, nail-biting, down-to-the-wire match-up. The only thing better is a close game that your beloved team wins. But the amount of money invested in sports teams is, in a large part, due to our obsession with winning. It is as if winning a game, or a championship, validates our worthiness. If some cities invested as much into transforming their schools as they do in subsidizing professional sports arenas, imagine the number of quieter, and lasting, success stories that would result.

How do you act on your own behalf and not be attached to outcome? It doesn't serve to be a relativist in relation to your aspirations. You are attached to results when you believe they will add to your life in a meaningful way. That is why it is more helpful to think about holding lightly to the particular outcome you want rather than practicing non-attachment. The challenge is to get perspective on, and distance from, your attachments.

If you really want something, set a high bar and go for it! Be directed and persistent in your actions. Then, develop a certain engaged detachment about how things unfold. Know that your goals will likely unfold in ways other than you imagine. And let that be interesting, not a problem.

When things don't work out the way you want, it can be difficult to have faith that, ultimately, things will turn out alright. You sometimes need external validation to feel OK about how you are doing. Everyone needs positive reinforcement. But it is not always available. And sometimes it is available but not in a way you recognize. By looking for the success or "the win," it can place you at a disadvantage, making it more difficult to skillfully act over time. This is why a cultural obsession with winning does not bring out the best in any of us, even when we "win."

It is sometimes difficult to know when something is working, if you are making progress and need to stay at it. Likewise, it can be hard to know when something is not working and it's time to let go and redirect your efforts. Most successful endeavors have had setbacks and disappointments. How do you know when to hang in there if things are not going according to plan? How do you stay invested without giving too much away? There is no best answer to these questions. But if you value effort over outcome, you will have greater confidence in your ability to answer them.

How to Act in the Face of Doubt

Gary left his job in the entertainment industry and took a year to travel around the world. This experience opened his eyes to how driven he had been in his career and how little joy it had brought him. He had focused exclusively on climbing the corporate ladder without reflecting on how to meaningfully get there. Gary now wanted a fundamentally different relationship to work, one that matched his clarified values. He decided that he could not return to his company. He now wanted to bring his skills to a company that made a positive impact in the world and valued its employees' well-being as central to its mission.

Gary discovered that his skills were not as transferrable as he hoped. He anticipated the need to work for a lower salary, but nothing was materializing that paid any stable salary whatsoever. He needed to earn an income that would help him live simply in New York City—no small task. Gary persisted and had some real possibilities. Yet after six months with no job offer, he was anxious and deflated.

Making a radical change in lifestyle, like Gary was trying to do, takes a leap of faith and persistence. This is true whether that change is primarily internal or external. There is often a crisis of faith. There are not ready-made models or opportunities. You must create them. When you most need encouragement it can be hard to find. At these times, it is important to know that you aren't alone. The feeling of being lost comes with the territory. It is easy to start telling yourself a story that other people have made these transitions more successfully and with greater ease. When this happens, the story becomes about your failure or your unworthiness. The story may be about fairness or unfairness. Be aware of these unhelpful stories that thwart your ability to stay the course.

Gary gradually built a small internet business in order to pay his bills while he continued to pursue a purposeful relationship to work. Gary did not initially view the work in his side business as meaningful. He actually experienced it as drudgery. But when he recognized that the business was a good fit for him at that moment, because it helped him accomplish other valued goals, he found meaning in it. He limited his time commitment to this business because he wanted to keep sight of working in the kind of company he envisioned. But he no longer resisted this work and even found it engaging at times.

This is an example of Gary practicing intentional action and learning to hold lightly to a particular outcome. He moved from feeling lost to honing his actions in ways that furthered his aspirations. As Gary practiced holding his desired outcomes lightly, he was better able to recognize and be heartened by changes he was gradually making and took further action to build on them. For over two years, he felt encouraged at times, yet discouragement was often just around the corner. During those two years, he continued to occasionally feel lost and, at times, wondered if his vision for the kind of life he wanted was unattainable. But he persisted; practicing direct reflection, taking small steps, and learning from the outcome. Gary came to appreciate the length of time it can take to lay the groundwork for pervasive, qualitative change. In so doing, he valued the small steps he took as he understood their importance.

Did Gary find a place in the kind of company he envisioned? He did, but not in the way he had imagined. Through trying to solve some issues with his internet company, he met some entrepreneurs with a creative model of delivering services. Gary found their work to be meaningful and, while they didn't have the finances to hire him, he now has a small stake in the company by providing his services to them. He is hopeful that the company will grow and, when it does, there will be a central place for him.

Focus on What's Here Right Now

Being an intentional actor means understanding where and when to act. The key to wise effort is to understand what is here for you right now. And, importantly, it means redirecting energy away from what is not possible at this moment in time. Sometimes you won't know what is here for you until you take action.

The following is a sequence to help you practice wise effort. First, take intentional action and put out, clearly, what you would like. Then pause and assess the results of your action. Take further intentional action in response to what is unfolding in the present moment. Don't be afraid to go for what you want. Don't hold back from investing your time and resources. Again, take a step and see the response that you get. Don't try to force a response. If you get a response in kind, take another step.

As an example, Gary expressed his desire to transfer his skills to a company he found inspiring and got rejected from all to which he applied. If he wanted to continue to pursue this dream he needed a new approach. What Gary discovered is true for many of us; finding a way to transfer skills often means we have to create opportunity.

Apply for your dream job. If you don't get it, pause and assess if taking further action—like pursuing education or gaining different experience—would be helpful or possible. If so, do so. Formal education, though, is often not as helpful as experience, and it can seem impossible to get the needed experience. Holding lightly to outcome often means exploring models of creating opportunity that are not obvious. Sometimes it takes multiple actions, over a longer period of time, to increase the chances of opportunity presenting itself.

Another example, you are dating someone who is available but who does not seem as enthusiastic as you are. How much time do you spend waiting to see if his or her interest changes? The answer depends on if you are in a state of waiting. If so, and you can't step out of this state, then it is often healthiest to step away before investing further. If you can hold lightly and be sincerely open to others who are fully present to you right now, there is no harm in seeing what unfolds with the person who doesn't share your enthusiasm. But, as will be seen later in the example of Dyanna it can be easy to fall into a state of waiting that interferes with meaningful action.

As a final example: What about an established relationship, an old friendship, or even a partnership, which has lost its closeness and is unhappy? How much do you keep investing? You don't take stepping away from a relationship which once worked lightly. But you can't keep acting with intention in a relationship if it is not mutual. There is no clear answer about whether to stay or leave, but the approach is the same. Take action by being clear about what you want. If you would like to reestablish closeness, aspire to it, communicate it clearly, and be willing to show up for it yourself. Take a small measurable step. Then see what comes back to you. If you take action and the other person responds, but not in the way you would like, then pause, reevaluate and take another step. Can you take small steps and build your way back to closeness together? When you approach the relationship in this way, you will both have greater clarity about whether this relationship can regain its intimacy.

We suffer when we take action to make something come about that we cannot control. When we don't get the result we want, we can feel helpless and thwarted. We can become angry and impatient. It can be easy to double down and try to make something happen or, through inaction, wait for something to happen. Neither of these two approaches is helpful.

Holding lightly is not the same as feigning disinterest or being noncommittal. Some people confuse holding lightly as a way of playing a situation— which is another way of holding tightly to a particular outcome. Holding tight to a desired outcome leads to distorting and misinterpreting information so that you can still hold onto what is not here for you. The belief that if you just keep trying harder—or that by waiting longer—it may come is a common misconception. It wastes far more time than the practice of holding lightly, feeling the pain of disappointment, and redirecting energy to the real possibilities that are right here now.

When your efforts are not met with the outcome you want, it is natural to feel disappointment. Disappointment can be overcome if you respond skillfully to it. A disappointing outcome is not a reflection on your character or a personal affront. As you develop practices around wise effort, you will have plenty of opportunity to experience disappointment and move on! Don't underestimate how important this practice is—experiencing the disappointment and moving on. How you respond to missteps and disappointments is key in being an effective actor. This is more important than initial successes.

When you are disappointed, you have the opportunity to examine your expectations. Expectations around outcomes you can't control impair your ability to take meaningful action. Have hopes, have vision—but let go of expectations. When you do, your mind is nimble and open to the greatest range of possibility.

When to Persist and When to Move On

Dyanna, a dynamic woman in her late twenties, had a best friend named Dan who was slightly older. She was in a state of waiting in her friendship with Dan. Close confidants, they knew each other for over one year and had never been romantic. They shared a sensibility and humor. When Dan traveled for work, he called Dyanna regularly. They supported each other's careers; often bouncing ideas off of each other. Dyanna wanted more from their relationship. She knew that Dan cared for her but didn't know if he had thought about taking their relationship to another level. After a year, when Dan had still not shown romantic interest, Dyanna told herself that she needed to start dating. When she did, she compared every person to Dan. As a result, no relationship had a chance to get out of the starting gate. Dyanna recognized that her feelings for Dan were limiting her. She did want the possibility of finding a partner—if not Dan, then someone else.

Dyanna held tightly to her fantasies about a different kind of relationship with Dan but took no action to see if it was possible. This not only kept her in a state of waiting, it also resulted in her friendship with him, which meant a lot to her, paling in comparison to her fantasies.

Dyanna recognized that she needed to take action in her relationship with Dan in order to know what was possible and move on if need be. Though it was difficult at first, she became willing to let go of fantasies of a romantic partnership in order to open to what was actually possible between them. Dyanna gathered the courage to tell Dan she was open to more than friendship with him. The conversation was awkward. Dan told Dyanna that he did love her and valued her friendship. He shared with her that he had questioned himself why he wasn't open to taking the relationship to another level. He just knew he didn't feel that it was the right step to take. He was grateful that what was unspoken was now out in the open between them. Dan hoped he wouldn't lose Dyanna as a dear friend. She told him she also valued his friendship and hoped they could remain friends.

Dyanna felt sadness—and also relief. Her deepest sadness was that she had kept herself in a state of waiting for nearly two years by valuing fantasy over what was real and here for her. Along with sadness, she also felt energized that she had taken action to free herself from the state of waiting. This intentional, and difficult, action ushered in sincere openness to other people. She could now imagine the possibility of a relationship with someone other than Dan.

Think about your life as the directed yet meandering river. Understand that this non-linear path is the very nature of a purposeful life. Value effort over outcome and you, like Gary, will come to appreciate the unpredictable way that your actions play out. Value what is here for you now and, like Dyanna, be willing to let go of fantasy if it keeps you from taking effective action. Dreams are high aspirations and often require persistent effort. Be clear on what you believe will bring you purpose, develop concrete goals, and take small steps toward them. Then remain open to the mystery of how life unfolds.

Chapter 13

What To Do When
You Are Stuck

*One had to take some action against fear when
once it had laid hold of one.*
Rainer Maria Rilke

Everyone gets stuck. The internal experience of being stuck is generally negative—that we are prevented from taking meaningful action. We feel most alive, creative, and purposeful when experiencing ourselves acting with volition. But viewing the state of stuck-ness as a problem encourages strategies that make us more stuck. Being stuck is only a problem if we cannot move through it. What we do in response to feeling stuck influences our ability to change the experience. It can be tempting to avoid action or distract ourselves from the discomfort of feeling stuck. Neither strategy is helpful. Taking meaningful action, *especially* when you are stuck, helps you acquire faith that you are the central actor in your life.

Just as turbulence is a natural part of being a passenger on an airplane, occasionally being stuck is an inevitable part of taking meaningful action. To be an effective actor you don't need perpetual ease of motion. If you had it, you probably would not be stretching yourself. Stuck-ness is not the same as non-movement. This is an important distinction because you may respond to the discomfort of non-movement with action that makes you stuck!

You can get stuck in two ways. First, you can get stuck by not acting intentionally; by acting in ways that hinder effective movement. This is often the case when you experience resistance, which is a special type of stuck-ness that will be discussed later. You can also become stuck because circumstances simply don't allow for effective action.

Both kinds of stuck-ness, hindering yourself or in response to external circumstances, require understanding. Feeling frustrated or thwarted does not promote understanding or help you act with intention. By placing awareness on the experience of stuck-ness, to understand it, actually shifts your experience of it. This simple practice, placing awareness, adds a degree of fluidity to the experience of feeling stuck. Becoming unstuck requires compassion, and gentle persistence.

First, try to understand whether your experience of being stuck is primarily internal or external. If the reasons for being stuck are external, then explore what, if anything, you can do about it at this particular moment in time. Do you need extra support or resources? Do you need to get more data before taking further action? If you are stuck primarily because of internal resistance, then the primary way through it is greater self-understanding and a commitment to keep showing up.

When Resistance is Behind Being Stuck

Internal resistance likely accounts for a large portion of the stuck-ness you experience. Resistance, as defined here, is an internal block from action. The block is within you. There may be very good reasons you are resisting taking action. Maybe you think you should do something that you don't really want to do. Or you wisely need to pause and understand the situation further before taking action. Sometimes the reasons stem from fears or doubts that need to be understood and addressed. Maybe resistance is a habitual response.

Whatever the reasons for resistance, if they are not understood, you experience yourself as unable to act on your behalf. Or, you do act, but it feels like you are dragging yourself, kicking and screaming, the entire time. Learning to identify the causes of your resistance, and moving through them, is empowering.

———

Jana felt like she had a good life. But in the past six months she had begun feeling ennui, a general sense of listlessness, that wasn't dissipating. She entered therapy with a desire to move beyond her comfort zone, to be more social and try new things. Doing so was a challenge for Jana because she was introverted and, while she had come far in feeling comfortable with herself, she still felt socially awkward. For the past few years Jana told herself that she preferred to stay home or have quiet evenings with one or two friends. And sometimes this was true. But she now recognized that it was also true that she avoided taking risks because she didn't like feeling uncomfortable and awkward. Avoidance was limiting her and caused more pain than the discomfort that she avoided.

Jana wanted to use therapy as a place to be held accountable to take steps toward her goals. She made concrete decisions and set out to take meaningful, but manageable, action toward being more social. She returned one session feeling deflated and upset with herself for "being lazy and having stupid reasons for not following through".

Instead of focusing on why she didn't do what she set out to do, we instead focused directly on the experience of resistance. Jana began with a "small, silly example" of taking steps to buy clothes. Most days she wore gym clothes and, while clothes were not a high priority to her, she wanted to dress in a way that gave an impression of putting her best foot forward. Her first action was to go online and look at different kinds of clothes to see which styles she might like wearing. She quickly felt overwhelmed by options. In addition to being overwhelmed by the sheer number of options, Jana also thought back to shopping experiences where she felt discouraged because designers didn't often create clothes for her body type. Exploring her experience of resistance more, when she imagined buying clothes online and needing to return some of them, she thought about having difficulty getting around to it. As she shared her mental gymnastics, it was understandable how she had trouble taking meaningful action.

As Jana unpacked her resistance to taking action, she could see how this silly example was not silly at all. It was significant and gave important information on how to move forward and act in ways that she could feel good about.

Jana and I shifted the way we worked for the next couple of weeks. I asked her to call me for ten minutes every day so that we could explore the experience of resistance closer in time to when she was experiencing it. Working in this way helped Jana understand that she experienced resistance differently at different times. It was also a good model for Jana to understand how she could create and modify her own strategies for moving through resistance whenever it arose.

Starting with the action of buying clothes that she enjoyed wearing, Jana extended this experience to more challenging social situations. Each new circumstance offered an opportunity for insights and further practice in working with resistance. Jana moved out of her comfort zone. She now experiences herself as more social, and socially skillful, than she once did.

The internal experience of resistance can stem from fear, self-doubt, or judgment. For Jana, it was her unspoken belief that she would ultimately fail which overwhelmed her as she approached taking small meaningful actions toward her goals. Resistance can arise out of simply not knowing how to proceed. It can come from difficulty in showing up for yourself when not feeling motivated. Resistance as an approach can become a habit in and of itself. Avoidance can take on a life of its own. And when it does, it hobbles your capacity to be the central actor in your life. When you don't understand your resistance, the sense of struggle persists. It becomes a cyclic relationship with stuck-ness.

I have worked with college students who had a habitual style of writing papers at the last minute. They felt resistance right up until there was imminent pressure of the deadline breathing down their neck. This relationship to deadlines is not uncommon. Resist as pressure mounts … feel uncomfortable about what needs to be done… discomfort leads to more resistance and avoidance … when there is no more perceived wiggle room to avoid, crank it out. Afterward there is often an experience of relief—of having dodged a bullet—exhaustion and slight elation. And there can also be regret afterward, a desire to have had just a little more time. If only there had been one more day the paper could have been really great!

Meaningful action can lay bare underlying roadblocks that have been hidden. So sometimes it is *because* you are practicing intentional action that you experience resistance. Meaningful action can reveal more about what you need to learn in order to take further steps toward your goals. This can be discouraging. You may feel resistance to the new information. It is important to meet disappointment with openness rather than resistance. Meet each new juncture as an opportunity to evaluate, to make new choices and to take new action.

Learning to let go of resistance allows for greater ease in life. Things that are challenging, or hard, don't need an added layer of resistance on top of them. Save your energy for struggles that are worth having. Sometimes deadlines do help to give an added push. But a habitual response of taking action forced by external pressure does not allow you to experience yourself as someone who can act intentionally.

If you believe you really want something but continue to feel resistance, this is the invitation to go deeper within yourself and understand what you are resisting. Importantly, it is an opportunity for you to practice joining with yourself in new ways.

Two Bad Habits that Keep You Stuck

Two habits that keep us stuck are *Distraction* and *Waiting for Inspiration*.

Distraction requires little explanation and we all have favorite ways of distracting ourselves. My home is never cleaner than when I'm facing deadlines.

I surf real estate and travel websites. What's important is to stay mindful of when we take action that serves more as distraction than meaningful action. Distraction as action makes it even more difficult to return and reengage.

Don't wait for inspiration! Inspiration, like deep happiness, comes in moments. You can help cultivate the conditions to feel inspired but you can't control its occurrence. It is helpful to have a practice of learning to take advantage of inspiration. And when it visits, strike while the iron is hot. When you are stuck, it can be tempting to wait until you feel inspired to move out of it. This waiting stance is a dead end. It is important to be compassionate with yourself when you are stuck. At the same time, gently prompt yourself to move out of the state of inertia. Recognize that waiting for the spirit to move you decreases the likelihood that the spirit will move you.

Does this mean that inspiration does not exist? Not at all. It is central to the creative process. The problem is waiting for it. You can't force inspiration to come to you. It is spontaneous. This might relieve you of feeling as if you *should* be inspired. At the same time, preparation is key to inspiration. When it comes, get a foothold in a way that allows for intentional action. Practicing good habits allows effective action when inspiration visits. Distracting yourself while waiting for inspiration does not.

One of my favorite maxims is Rudyard Kipling's writing mantra, "Drift, wait, and obey." While this described the writing process for Kipling, it can describe any creative engagement. Here, drifting is a state in which you allow your creative process to be at the forefront. It is different from spacing out or getting distracted. It describes a state of non-directed openness to possibility. Kipling himself would go on long walks in the English countryside, calling this process *hatching*.

The waiting Kipling refers to is not a passive stance. It is not a state of waiting described earlier which is the result of resistance. Rather, Kipling's waiting is allowing the possibility of inspiration to show itself. It showed itself because he *persistently* showed up for writing. When ideas spontaneously came to him he referred to his inspiration as his *daemon* being in charge.

When his *daemon* was in charge he wrote feverishly. He took advantage of these states because he knew they came only intermittently.

Obey means follow the energy. It is not a dictatorial kind of obey but, instead, a call to show up for yourself. When you get inspired, for goodness sake, take advantage of it. Inspiration is a gift that should not be wasted! Even if you don't know the best next step to take, take a step. This helps you engage more meaningfully with the experience of internal movement that is inspirational. Practices in intentional action include cultivating the conditions to both find inspiration and to act on it when it comes.

Practices That Help You Get Unstuck

These are three helpful practices when you are stuck. The first is "showing up." The second is "take baby steps." And the third is "follow the energy."

Showing up means having a commitment to stay present to what is difficult or uncomfortable. It means not avoiding. It means coming back to something again and again. That term paper that is avoided until there is no perceived alternative? Try a different approach. Show up for it when it is first assigned. Make it an interesting experiment and take more ownership of the process. You have the opportunity to write creatively in a new way. Make it your paper, written in your voice. An authentic written voice takes reflection and multiple passes. An all-nighter fueled by pots of coffee does not lend itself to the creative process. While this approach might be necessary at times, it often isn't.

How do you show up for something that you are resisting? Can you just evoke some powerful self-discipline? Tell yourself to buck up and push through it? Can you power through with a sheer force of will? Maybe, but not likely. At least not beyond the short term. Trying to force yourself can make you more frustrated and resistant.

Showing up, again and again, requires an openness to your resistance without giving into it. Showing up includes taking steps toward a goal. It is through ongoing intentional action that resistance is overcome. It is by gently and persistently asking yourself to imagine, and then commit to, the next small step. The next step does not need to be the *right step*. Let go of the idea of right or best step! It just needs to be a step of sincere presence and effort. The practice of taking just one more step gives you faith in yourself and frees up energy. Don't get down on yourself if you feel resistance to the next step. Yet don't give in to the resistance either.

To continue with the example of the college paper, as soon as it is assigned, spend ten minutes jotting down ideas in a notebook. Don't ask anything more of yourself. A few days later show up in another way. Try looking up half a dozen references, allowing this to take only twenty minutes. Don't ask anything else of yourself. A day later, pick up that list of references and ask yourself, "Which of these, if any, sounds interesting to me?" If one stands out, get that reference and read it right away. Don't ask anything more of yourself. The next day, spend ten minutes of thinking of the next step. Don't ask anything more of yourself. And so on. If at any point, you feel inspired, then by all means ask more of yourself!

Take baby steps means take action in small, measurable ways. It takes skill and practice to formulate meaningful incremental steps. However small the step, action in the right direction counters the inertia of feeling stuck. When you are stuck, you might need help with understanding how to formulate baby steps. If this is the case, getting the right kind of help is a very effective incremental step to take. Learning to identify and take baby steps toward your goals is an invaluable lifelong practice.

When you look back at how you achieved your highest aspirations, it may seem like you took major leaps at key moments. Those moments will leave indelible prints in your memories. But these leaps were possible because of a foundation of small steps. If you consistently show up by taking small, incremental steps, you will effectively move toward what matters most to you.

Follow the energy means that when something energizes you, listen to it. The experience of stuck-ness is one of constriction. It doesn't help to meet constriction with force. When you do the constriction gets tighter. For example, if you have a habit of finishing assignments because of external pressure, the experience teaches you nothing about being an intentional actor. Acting solely in response to deadlines doesn't encourage you to act in engaged and creative ways. Countering constriction with openness changes the experience. Finding pockets of energy, or interest, is an opening experience that helps you meet the resistance. If you can channel energy into movement toward what you are resisting, it will help you take the next small step more easily. Following your energy is important because it helps to counter internal resistance.

That same college paper? Following the energy means taking time when the assignment is first given to choose a topic that interests you. If there is no curiosity up-front, resistance is nearly guaranteed. If you are interested in the topic, you can tap into energy which helps you access the ideas that stuckness is inhibiting.

Now you have a topic that interests you and you have researched it. It is time to start writing, but you encounter the old familiar resistance. Can you infuse energy into the experience? Walk in your room and say out loud the important themes you want to include in your paper. Sing them. Break down writing the paper into small incremental goals and ask yourself only to show up twenty minutes at a time. Knowing beforehand what you are asking of yourself, and having it be manageable, helps you bring energy to the experience. Create a list of activities you enjoy, that are energizing, and take breaks for these activities. Make plans to go out with friends after writing a page or two. Discover new, quiet places to write that are not associated with the experience of resistance. The most important point is that you bring awareness to the process and think of ways to infuse the act of writing with openness and energy.

—⁓—

By bringing awareness to the internal experience of being stuck, you are able to bring skills to the process that will help you move through it. Counter bad habits, like distraction and waiting for inspiration, with intentional practices in action. These include showing up, taking small steps, and channeling your energy for the task at hand. Taking meaningful action, especially when you feel stuck, gives you a powerful sense of volition and confidence in your ability to act on your behalf. Intentional action transforms the experience of struggle to that of empowerment.

Part V

Allowing

Chapter 14

The Wisdom of Making Space
for What is Here

Gratitude bestows reverence, allowing us to encounter everyday epiphanies,
those transcendent moments of awe that change forever
how we experience life and the world.
John Milton

The fifth foundation of an intentional life is allowing, which is the act of letting be; letting experience unfold without interfering. Experience is disallowed when we try to change it as it is happening. Allowing is a state loaded with possibility. It welcomes all that is happening within you—thoughts, feelings and physical sensations—as well as what is happening around you. When you allow experience to unfold you have tamed the habit of trying to control it. You let experience come to you, aligning with the external world in a more collaborative relationship. It is not that you don't think or act, but thinking and acting do not dominate the experience. Allowing enables you to more creatively join yourself with the external world. You become part of the experience and let it impact you—just as you impact it.

Allowing is surprisingly difficult to do. For many of us it is a radical act. For years I could not step back from a habitual style that valued constant do-ing. I eventually recognized that I had an unarticulated belief that I constantly had to work hard, even when it wasn't necessary, in order to feel purposeful or deserving of abundance. I had difficulty allowing good things to come my way unless I had, in my mind, earned it. To this day, when fortunate events happen, without my having had to try hard, I can still feel surprised. I still remind myself that this is how it can be. I now believe in the benevolent and helpful forces in the world that are waiting to be tapped.

An important intentional practice that lays the groundwork for allowing experience to unfold is noticing when you are disallowing. You may think that you are trying to understand experience while, in reality, you are disallowing it to be as it is. Watch your mind's moment-to-moment interruptions of experience as they are occurring.

When you first try to practice allowing it can seem like it runs counter to the ability to be volitional. This is because allowing is unfamiliar and can be mistaken for passivity. But in reality, allowing is a vitally active stance. In fact, your capacity to reflect, make decisions, and take action is more flexible and creative when occurring in the open space of allowing—because you are in a synergistic relationship with the world around you.

While allowing does include noticing, it is more than that. It is an all-encompassing opening to experience. It is a state you naturally arrive at from practicing in the other four core areas of intention. When you arrive, notice where you have come to and volitionally join with the benefits that come with it. While allowing is not something you strive for, you can sow the seeds for the experience by an active receptivity to what is here for you right now.

The Anywhere-But-Here Nature of the Mind

Going on meditation retreats throws into sharp relief how difficult it is to allow. Meditation provides the opportunity to witness thoughts that rise up to meet every experience. I was on a week-long retreat with nothing to do other than to let experience unfold. The entire retreat was in silence. No eye contact was made between retreatants as a way of heightening awareness of our minds. The retreat was structured around forty-five minute periods of meditation—alternating between sitting and walking meditation. Other than meditating there were two meals, a snack, and one talk in the evening given by a teacher. That was it, from 6:00 a.m. to 9:00 p.m. What there was "to do" was notice and allow experience.

Even as I set my intention to simply allow, and was having brief moments of doing just that, I'd quickly shift to wondering how I could extend this experience to my day-to-day life in New York City. In almost all of the meditations I spent time thinking about the future—calculating how many more meditations were left in the day, wondering about the lunch menu, thinking about where I would go for the next walking meditation. I did this rather than simply allowing the experiences of the meditation to unfold, experiencing lunch as I was eating it, and choosing where to have my walking meditation after the bell sounded the end of the previous meditation. The many ways my mind left the present experience could fill countless pages that nobody would want to read. Uninterrupted experience is far more interesting—and fleeting.

Allowing doesn't mean that you don't ask questions. Instead it means knowing what questions can be answered at any particular moment. It means recognizing which questions are helpful, and that those questions can often be answered best if you allow experience to unfold.

Allowing doesn't mean that you don't ever take action to try to change the course of what is happening. It does mean getting clear for yourself what, if anything, you want to do or can be done. It means that even when you try to change things, you remain receptive while doing so. A practice in allowing teaches you that you often don't have to think so hard about taking action because, by patiently allowing experience, the best course of action gets revealed. The revelation comes from within you, from a place that is familiar but not often accessed.

Practices in allowing are not intended to eradicate the mind's mark on experience. But allowing does slow down the automaticity of interrupting experience. As you develop your capacity to allow experience uninterrupted, it feels good and it feels spacious. With time, it feels transformative because you recognize how much is here for you that you didn't know before. By allowing experiences to unfold, they are more impactful and meaningful.

Exercise: A Helpful Way to Let Go

This can be a powerful exercise to help you set your intention to let go. It is a visual reminder that you can practice choice as to whether to cling to something or let it go. What you choose to let go can be situations, beliefs, anger, judgments, stories – anything that you believe is getting in the way for you.

First, close your eyes and notice your breath for at least a full minute. Let go of asking yourself any questions. Simply watch the breath as it enters and leaves our body. After the minute has passed, ask yourself directly, "What do I want to let go of?" or "What would help me to let go of?"

Write down what comes to you on a small scrap of paper. If multiple things come to you, write them down on several scraps of paper.

Put these scraps into a metal bowl. Close your eyes and set an intention to let these things go in your mind, your heart and your life. Put a match to the scraps of paper and watch them burn. (If there are multiple scraps, open a window!)

The More You Let Go, the More That Awaits You

Letting be requires Letting go: Letting go of what you believe you need to be happy; Letting go of wanting to be other than you are; Letting go of wanting others to be different; Letting go of attachment to things; Letting go of beliefs about how things should be; Letting go of stories; Letting go of fear; Letting go of waiting for the conditions to be right for you to be happy.

It is not as if you, literally, excise the attachments you are holding onto. Instead, start with a sincere willingness to try, in your mind's eye, letting these things go. What feelings and thoughts come up as you imagine letting go of an attachment? What, if anything, gets in the way of letting go—even in your imagination? Practice imagining letting go over and over again. Then, after imagining letting go, practice concretely letting go of some of the things that clutter your life and your mind.

Letting go might mean finding ways you can simplify your life from unnecessary material things. Our culture is one that is destructively consumptive. As a participant in the culture, you may unknowingly participate in a way of living that is unsustainable for the planet. Letting go of excess is a practice that enriches your life as well as the lives of all beings on the planet.

Bring the practice of letting go into your closest relationships. Bring it to the things that are the most important to you. Because what you hold most dear, especially these things, you can hold tightly. Try to loosen that hold with the practice of letting go. Holding what you most value lightly enriches those relationships. Letting go of attachment to what matters most is radical, seemingly paradoxical, and allows for greater depth of loving.

If you have a practice in letting go, you'll witness how frequently your mind can hold a tight grip. Before having a practice, you may not have noticed what your mind clings to, but it affects you. For example, one of my practices in letting go is trying to notice when reflection turns into overthinking, and to let go of the habit of overthinking because it doesn't add any clarity to the situation. Sometimes I'll say to myself, out loud, "Is there any thought that would help me now? If not, can I lay down my thoughts around this?". The act of trying to let go reinforces a deeper understanding of what serves your interests and what doesn't.

Sometimes you will find that you are unable to let something go. Maybe someone has hurt you tremendously. Maybe you've acted in a way that caused regret. Maybe you have a deep belief that what you need to be happy lies outside of yourself. Maybe you define yourself by others' perceptions of you.

This realization of your inability to let go is not cause for getting down on yourself. Instead, it is a reason for being compassionate toward yourself.

Because holding onto pain, anger, and longing causes further suffering. Holding onto narrow definitions of your worth causes suffering. It may be that you cannot do anything about it at the moment. Yet still have letting go as an aspiration. Have a willingness to test out, over and over, your ability to let go.

It helps to ask yourself, sincerely, "Can I let this go right now?" And, if not, "What, if anything, can help me let this go?" "What would it look like if I let this go?"

The paradox of letting go of what your mind is grasping, like the paradox of allowing, is that the more you are able to let go, the more that becomes available to you.

Allowing Leads to the Experience of Flow

A powerful type of allowing occurs while in the state of flow. Flow is a unique state of absorption, of being completely immersed in an action or experience. Out of the state of flow comes clarity, creativity, and sometimes profound insight.

A common phrase *go with the flow* means accepting experience—not resisting it. The person going with the flow is often thought of as being easygoing. This definition of flow captures the quality of nonresistance in the state of flow. However, it misses the importance of persistent effort that is required for the heightened focus and preparedness that makes the state of flow so special.

People who experience flow states often have practices in concentration and awareness. In the state of flow, your sense of self is lost; there is complete absorption with the experience itself and you are not separate from it. Your sense of time changes with an awareness only of the present moment. Qualities of knowledge and clarity are heightened. When flow is experienced in conjunction with intentional practices, it deepens your capacity to direct your life in powerful ways.

Paul was under extraordinary pressure because his company had been subsumed by a larger company. He didn't know if there was a place for him in the new company. The executives who believed in him were unable to protect him because they did not, themselves, know what would happen. In the midst of intense stress and uncertainty, Paul had an unexpected experience of flow during a work presentation.

He was asked to go on a retreat with executives from both the old and new company. He welcomed the opportunity, hoping it was a sign that there would be a place for him in the restructuring. He felt he had one chance to make an impression, which led to tremendous internal pressure. While preparing for the presentation Paul had high levels of anxiety and began to ruminate. Doubt creeped in regarding whether he could rise to the occasion—even though he knew his material inside and out and was a skillful speaker. Paul's anxiety became so intense that the thought of making the presentation became aversive.

Fortunately, Paul was asked to present to the group early in the retreat. His discomfort had become so intense that he shifted to a place of "not caring anymore." He just wanted it to be over. This was the best thing that could have happened because it enabled Paul to get out of his own way. He was able to focus and approach the material he knew so well with ease. He forgot the weight he had placed on his performance and experienced flow from beginning to end. The audience responded enthusiastically.

In telling me about this experience, Paul wondered how he could allow himself to have these experiences more readily. Could he get to a point of "not caring" what others thought, in a healthy way, without going through prolonged intense anxiety and self-doubt? Bringing this experience to his awareness, Paul utilized it as a springboard for focusing on the process of allowing things to unfold. He realized that learning to care less, not out of feeling exhausted from caring too much, was a path to greater authenticity and showing the best of himself. He now committed to creating these states more often, regardless of where he landed in the new company.

For thousands of years practitioners of Buddhism have practiced mindfulness to welcome flow-like states. Rituals in different religions have a common goal of cultivating these experiences of connection to something greater. These rituals, involving repetition, concentration, and sensory awareness, were intended to help a person move to a heightened state of awareness. This awareness may have been of greater connection to God or, in Buddhism, a breakdown in the experience of self and other. In the 1960s, the concept of flow became popularized in Western psychology. Like flow states in religious ritual, they described states where time stands still, we are less aware of ourselves, and aware of being part of something larger. Actions taken while in flow are intrinsically rewarding. What these understandings of flow states have in common is the importance of having practices that cultivate them. In other words, persistent effort and skill seed the conditions for flow.

Flow states have a positive impact on the quality of your life—don't leave them to chance! They allow you a more direct relationship with your interior and so lead to the experience of authenticity. If flow states are directed toward your highest aspirations, they are transformative.

Some people seek out flow experiences for their own sake. This can foster a continual pursuit of experiences, followed by *"Now what?"* We can become flow zealots, perpetually seeking the next peak experience at the expense of moment-to-moment of life as it is, leading to discontent. We can lose sight of engaging meaningfully with all our internal states and external experiences.

It is ongoing practices in intentionality that seed both peak flow experiences and authenticity.

An intentional life does not preference flow experiences over other ways of experiencing. You may personally prefer effortless states of absorption, but they are not central to the practices of living intentionally. Instead, they are a rewarding byproduct.

What's important is to try to bring a quality of awareness to all of your internal states: flow states, grappling states, fear states, contentment states, confused states, clarity states, and somewhere-in-between states. Heightened awareness to all states is what leads to ownership of your life.

Allow Others to Have Their Own, Unique Experience

Just as you practice allowing your own experience to unfold, practice it in relation to others. When you make room for others' experience you are seeding the conditions of greater connection and intimacy.

Parents understand how difficult it can be to allow children to learn from their own experiences. There can be a fine line between guiding children and interfering with their experience. It is so important that children have room to practice create their own experience—reflecting, making decisions and taking action—and learning from what unfolds. It's understandable that parents don't want their kids to suffer negative consequences from their choices or actions. Yet without the opportunity to practice, children can't learn to shape their own lives. The most valuable guidance, within parameters and in age-appropriate ways, is allowing children to test out for themselves the contingencies of their reflections, choices, and actions.

~

Jane and her ten-year-old son, Stefan, regularly battled over his homework. Stefan sometimes watched TV before his homework was finished, which was against the rules. Jane would ask if Stefan had finished his homework and, if he hadn't, he'd respond angrily. She would threaten to take away his electronics which escalated his anger. On one or two occasions, he told her he had finished when he hadn't. When she found out, she became angrier. Beneath her anger was a fear that Stefan's behavior would generalize into a larger pattern of lying.

When Jane came for help with parenting Stefan, one of the first things I asked was what happened in the past when Stefan got to school and his homework wasn't done. Jane told me that this never happened, not once. He was an exceptional student and his occasional challenges at school were behavioral, not academic. I asked what her concerns were around Stefan having his own experience of taking responsibility for homework. What was her fear of his going to school one time without having it done? Could she allow him to experience those consequences? Since Stefan had a style of getting down on himself when he didn't excel, it was my guess that he'd be pretty unhappy about not having his homework finished. Jane's fear was that it would be a slippery slope, like Stefan's lying. In her mind, if Stefan didn't turn in his homework once, it was just a matter of time until he would stop caring about his school performance. Her fear-based response was fueling arguments between them.

I asked Jane to think of a time when she didn't, or nearly didn't, meet a deadline at work. Interestingly, she perked up as she shared her resourcefulness at meeting the necessary deadlines. She thrived under pressure and prided herself on her ability to get things in under the wire. When thinking about it this way, Jane recognized that she wasn't allowing Stefan to learn to monitor his own progress. Her fear loosened its grip and she could make more room for Stefan. Jane should still monitor his homework. Yet an allowing practice for Jane meant holding more lightly to how she does that.

Several months later, Stefan continued to complete his assignments. Jane actively practiced allowing by letting Stefan experiment with how he approached his job (school). Jane recognized the importance of communicating more frequently to Stefan around what he did well. Homework was important but outcome was not the only important thing. Jane now tried to guide Stefan to be more supportive of himself. His high expectations got in the way of his finding satisfaction in the effort he put into his work. Jane recognized that how he felt about himself as he worked was more important than a homework assignment.

Jane's practice of allowing Stefan to learn about shaping his own life ushered in greater ease between them. This is a benefit of allowing room for the other's experience in all relationships.

Chapter 15

At the End of the Search
is Abundance

*The universe is full of magical things patiently waiting for
our wits to grow sharper.*
Eden Phillpotts

The Rewards of an Intentional Life

"I'm trusting a state of being I'm not accustomed to, now that I'm convinced it's there. It is a part of myself I haven't before accessed in this way."

"I *want* to trust myself because it is clear now that I can trust what's there. And, without being self-conscious about it, I can give myself the opportunity to approach things differently."

"There is a kind of "just-enough" conscious awareness to allow me to dip down into aspects of myself I don't generally access. I feel more "me." The external world is responding to it, to me! I once thought self-analysis was the most important kind of knowing. But this is a different knowing, a deep awareness of myself and the world without so much thinking. I understand how I can move in alignment with myself, and the world, more of the time."

"It's like putting a puzzle together—the pieces that I did not think belonged to me now fit perfectly into this new way of experiencing myself."

Above are descriptions of the experience of living in a state of abundance. A thread that runs through them is a clear awareness of transformation. There is a sense of having arrived at a *place that has always existed*. Like the metaphor of life as the long, meandering river, eventually meeting up with the ocean—transformation is a return to our most authentic version of ourselves. We just didn't know it before or understand that we could access it through our own wise effort.

The pillars of intentional living explored in this book lay the groundwork for the experience of abundance, which presents itself when you know how to look. You can only arrive at abundance when you stop striving. It is this state of abundance that brings joy and makes life precious.

The qualities of residing in the state of abundance include a sense of plenitude, volition, and gratitude.

Plenitude is the experience of being full or complete. You experience plenitude when you know that you are whole and worthy just as you are. The same goes for what is happening externally. You have a sense that things are just as they need to be. This is true even in times of upheaval and even as you take action to change the conditions that exist. You experience a sense of possibility and of being ready to receive good things. In this state, there is a keen awareness of what is here right now and happiness with this realization. Inherent in this experience is a profound sense of contentment and purpose.

The experience of plenitude may be difficult to access in times of turmoil and great uncertainty. But it is precisely at these times that we have the opportunity to look with fresh eyes and discover new ways of living that are sustainable, in healthy collaboration with the needs of the planet. Misguided cultural views of abundance have caused great disparity and depletion of natural resources. Practicing intention opens you to the experience of plenitude that is not based on material wealth. You have an awareness that you don't need what you once thought you did. This awareness is freeing. You also want others to have the same experience of plenitude.

Having volition means that you experience yourself as having agency, able to make choices and act in a way that serves your interests. Living with intention, you understand that your interests are intimately bound to the well-being of others. Volition means that whatever circumstances you are in, no matter how challenging, you can still perceive and exercise choice, which is a powerful awareness. When you act with volition, your actions are influenced and initiated from within. They are not dependent on the immediate external environment because you recognize that what is here now will also pass. Along with this sense of greater agency, you develop an increased awareness of individual responsibility, a responsibility to your core values, to your own well-being, and to the well-being of others.

Gratitude is the experience of being thankful, the state of appreciation for what is here right now. You can cultivate a state of gratitude without waiting to feel grateful for something in particular. Choose to place your awareness on what you feel grateful for. Give more attention and put more energy into what you have that is bountiful over what is missing. The state of gratitude amplifies your subjective sense of well-being. Expressing gratitude to others generates good feelings and has a positive influence on your relationships.

The "Aha" of Not-A-Problem

The recognition of the state of abundance is often expressed as an "aha" moment. It is as if the lights have gone on and you recognize something that was there all along.

The radical shift that comes with living in a state of abundance is that what were once problems are no longer problems. This is a powerful awareness. The state of abundance allows you to embrace challenges rather than push them away or push through them. You can bring the same internal quality to all of your experiences and allow all experience to enrich you.

Teresa beautifully described the "aha" of recognizing that she could transform the experience of struggle:

"It's an awareness that's available to me much of the time now. And it enables me this kind of real time feedback. I'm like, 'What's happening? Where am I inside?' For example, today, I was in the conference room working and was getting too revved up. I was able to notice it in real time and take a few minutes to shift gears inside.

"And it extends to home. Last weekend I felt the effects of a really stressful week—month, actually. On Friday I had a really good night's sleep. I woke up Saturday feeling good but had a kind of a hangover from stress. I had downloaded a couple of apps to help Alan [Teresa's son] learn algebra. Alan was whiny and unappreciative. I could feel myself getting cranky and had an awareness of this low-level irritability. Yet, unlike in the past, I just said, 'Alan, I have to take a break and do something else for half an hour and then I'll come back.' I went outside and just putzed around. After half an hour I came back and was fine. This is such a departure from how I operated in the past. In the past, I would have been cranky and struggling and snapping.

"Now, difficult feelings still come up, but I touch base with myself naturally, automatically. "What's happening inside?" My internal tools are maybe the same as they were a year ago. The difference is I now trust myself to shift more quickly out of situations that I had seen as a problem. Now, problems aren't even problems! I can intervene and tweak … instead of having to go into major problem-solving mode which was the only response available to me in the past."

Teresa is referring to a qualitatively different experience that comes from her newfound ability to tap into a persistent internal awareness. She describes breaking through to something that has always been there. There has been a major perceptual shift that infuses all of her experience. Teresa describes this state as one in which she is more consistently and naturally present. She is aware of her internal states while, at the same time, is less self-preoccupied. This is important and often misperceived. A state of heightened self-awareness is not self-involved, quite the opposite. In this state Teresa is centered within herself while also more aware of her surroundings. She has greater clarity and volition over how to respond to her shifting internal states as well as to the external environment. She is still at times reactive to external events. The radical shift is that, in this state of abundance, Teresa is now able to tap into an internal awareness feedback loop and has greater choice in how she responds. In this way, what were once problems are no longer problems.

Teresa gave another example. She was recently thrown for a loop when her wife, Joanne, who didn't work outside the home, applied for a job and told Teresa after the fact. "She jumped from the brainstorming phase to 'Boom, I'm going to get a job.'"

Teresa was upset that Joanne hadn't first explored with Teresa the implications for the family if she went back to work. "Then I went through the day, literally, asking myself 'What am I reacting to?' 'This is how Joanne does things—not in steps like I would, but all in. So, what am I reacting to?' This question helped me wind down. I got home and wasn't angry. I was still upset and, to be honest, I had some judgment. I had thoughts like 'This is a selfish thing for her to do right now. The kids have been growing up with an engaged mom. We both are engaged, but she is always there, and they depend on this. There's going to be less of her available to them and the change will be abrupt.' I went through a couple of days with these thoughts.

"But with access to this more constant awareness, I now had important feedback available. 'I am angry' 'I am projecting onto the kids what they might go through.' 'Am I actually reacting to how this will be difficult for me?' As I was thinking in this new way, I was understanding, in a profound way, that all these things were manageable. Maybe better than the word manageable, there's more space ... there's room for everything. By the end of the weekend I felt like I still had an opinion on the matter—but it felt respectful of Joanne and her happiness. It felt healthy. I was able to see my way through to 'You know the kids will adjust, this is what happens.' And I was even able to see that I have a little more work to do around my judgment." (Teresa laughs good-naturedly at herself).

Teresa knows that even with her newfound experience of abundance, there will always be a need for an ongoing commitment to practice intention.

But now she also has clear recognition of what is available right now, along with a sense of greater spaciousness. Teresa's capacity to tap into this internal spaciousness—which is a manifestation of abundance—led to her wanting it for others, especially her wife. She recognized that, in an important way, it didn't matter what adjustments needed to be made if Joanne returned to work. What mattered was that Joanne felt free to pursue her own way of being authentic.

Another "aha" for Teresa was the recognition that it is *because* of these moments of constriction and struggle—perceived from the state of abundance—that she is able to experience new possibilities. What is radical and empowering is that she has a sense of how to transform the experience of struggle and unease, and this awareness brings deep happiness. Teresa recognizes her capacity to love herself, others, and her life more unconditionally.

Abundance is not mastering the external conditions of your life or your responses to what is happening. It is instead tapping into your ability to reflect, choose, and act in new ways. In Teresa's transformed way of living, she views challenges as opportunities for "data points" in how her life has radically shifted and how she can continue to evolve.

"It is really interesting ... really helpful ... to see how the same experience can be received with a much more insightful overlay, in a sense that this is who I am now. In the past it was, 'You have to do this to overcome.' I was reacting to externalities. I now have this profound awareness that it doesn't have to be this way. All situations that were once upsetting are now like experiments. I'm seeing things through a very different lens. It's amazing."

Final Thoughts

Practice Intention for the Benefit of All

L iving an intentional life is a means of flourishing as a human being. As we live intentionally, we seek to thrive in our conditions as they exist right now. This book is intended to guide you toward deepening your own comprehensive foundation for living. It is an ethics that addresses not only your personal concerns but the concerns of our time. Historically, it has never been clearer that they are part and parcel of the same thing.

Readers of *An Intentional Life: Five Foundations of Authenticity and Purpose* may recognize Buddhist practices in these pages, practices which are a beautiful systemic framework that transform lives. They are not the only path. All paths have in common heartfelt individual inquiry, intentional practices, engagement with the concerns of our time, and tolerance of different ways of addressing ultimate concerns.

If you stay on this path you are committing to not only your own personal welfare but to the well-being of all humans. How you place your awareness, reflect, make choices, and act has repercussions not only for yourself but for others. Intentional practices transform your life, and the world, when they are rooted in compassion. When you practice intentionality in all areas of your personal world, you are doing your part to act on behalf of the world.

This book lays out the five building blocks of intentional living. While you develop practices in these five core areas—awareness, reflecting, choosing, acting, and allowing—you will also approach the practices in the spirit of intention. The spirit of intention offers the key to staying on the overarching path to intentional living. In other words, intentionality operates on a micro- and macro-level at the same time. It infuses the moments of your life with meaning that transforms you and, potentially, those around you. The spirit of intention motivates you to continue to practice. It focuses your attention, encourages reflection, wise choices and action. It gives you clarity on how and when to take action.

Carve out time for intentional practices. Protect that time as sacrosanct. Allow the practices to gradually permeate all aspects of your life.

If you choose to stay on this path, it requires a degree of seriousness—which is only fitting for a commitment to your ultimate concerns. A commitment to living intentionally may mean making difficult decisions. Please don't let this scare you off. You cannot embody what you most highly value if you don't use what matters most as a basis for your choices and actions.

Find ways to continue on this very personal path. In this digital world, you have access to a wonderful range of materials that can support your practices. Take time and find resources that support and deepen your intentional lifestyle. It can be challenging to separate tools that overstate ways to make your life better from tools that help you live with greater intention.

Ask important questions along the way: "How is this for me?" "Can it add to my ability to live more intentionally?" If you think a tool might be helpful, approach it with intention and test it out.

The digital community does not replace the benefits of physically joining others to support each other on their individual paths. You may have the same question that many people do, "Now what?" "Where do I find support in my daily life to live in this way?" If there is no visible community to support you on this path, build it yourself. There are many people trying to find support in being authentic. Meet them. Cultivate relationships with them. The tools and supports you find helpful will organically change as you understand your path to intentional living on deeper and more subtle levels.

As you become increasingly adept at navigating your internal landscape and directing your life, take pleasure in your ability to skillfully bring intentionality to everything you do. Enjoy trusting your informed intuition to continue to guide you. Savor the abundance that comes from living in this way—and generously share it with others.

List of Intentional Practices

Chapter 1 Practices: How to Make Core Values Central in Your Life

Awareness:
- Become aware of two or three personal core values which resonate for you.
- Can you bring these core values into your awareness more of the time—at work and in your personal relationships?
- Notice when you are with people who share, and do not share, your core values. Notice the difference in your experience.

Reflect:
- Of your core values, which ones would be the same no matter what you were doing in your life?
- Think about how you manifest your core values in all areas of your life, especially in areas of most importance to you.
- Reflect on where you have difficulty bringing your core values into your life. What might get in the way?

Choose:
- Make decisions that reflect your core values.
- Choose to define your core values concretely so that they can help shape your decisions.
- Choose not to invest time or energy in situations that are in misalignment with your core values.

Act:
- Create a plan with clear steps to manifest your core values. Take an action to implement them daily.
- Cultivate relationships with people who live in alignment with their own personal core values.

Chapter 2 Practices: How to Actively Cultivate Well-Being

Awareness
- Place attention on how you experience well-being. How do you know when you feel it?
- Place greater attention on what you feel gratitude for and what is right about your life.
- Notice what brings positive emotions and what helps you let go of negative emotions.

Reflect
- Reflect upon activities that promote a sense of well-being and make time for them.
- Reflect on the kinds of thoughts that lead to the experience of positive feelings.
- Think about how to bring greater appreciation to the things you value most.

Choose
- Choose to take breaks from negative news and electronics.
- Choose to focus on yours and others' efforts for positive change in the world.
- Make choices with your time in ways that produce a sense of well-being—including time alone and with others.
- Choose to give more time to relationships that are mutually supportive.

Act
- Take care of your body by movement, exercise, and eating healthy food.
- Make social plans more often with people that value you for who you are and aspire to be.
- Practice types of self-care that are soothing and nurturing.
- Communicate appreciation for the people in your life right now.

Chapter 3 Practices: How to Have a Healthy Relationship to Your Desires

Awareness:
- Notice which desires get a lot of head space and energy.
- Be aware of self-judgment around your desires.
- Notice moments of contentment; when there is nothing that you desire.

Reflect:
- Reflect on ways that you can practice a healthy relationship to your desires.
- Think about when stepping back from a desire feels like a deprivation.
- Think about ways to enjoy desires that are in alignment with your core values.

Choose:
- Make healthy choices around desires.
- Choose to spend less time in thoughts about desires. Instead, make room for enjoying them.
- Choose to make desire for more money and material things less central to your day to day life.

Act:
- Have fun, be sexual, enjoy good drink and food, treat yourself.
- Step back from desires that have become habits or cravings (e.g., excessive shopping, drinking, working, etc.)
- Be creative. Find new ways to fulfill desires.

Chapter 4 Practices: The Importance of Pausing More

Awareness:
- Notice and appreciate the precious still moments when you are not lost in thought.
- Notice when your awareness leaves what you are doing in the present moment.
- Notice that moment you bring yourself back to the present moment.

Reflect:
- Begin each morning imagining how to create pauses throughout the course of your day.
- Think about what breaks from your routine enrich you most. How can you create more time for these?
- Reflect on circumstances that make it challenging to pause. How can you encourage stillness in these moments?

Choose:
- Choose to incorporate pauses throughout your day that help you feel centered.
- Choose to shut off your phone and step away from the internet for periods during the day, every day.
- Make lifestyle choices that allow you to take breaks from routine. These breaks are fertile ground for creativity.

Act:
- Take a moment to pause between one task and moving on to the next.
- Practice daily mindful awareness of your breath (see the practice in this chapter).
- Take vacations, use your personal days, take time off when you are sick, and make plans with people who enrich your life. Meditate, practice yoga, write in a journal.

Chapter 5 Practices: How to Shape
What Makes You Tick

Awareness:

- Notice the physical experience of different emotional states: anticipation, anger, ease, excitement, sadness, fear, anger, happiness, annoyance, joy.
- Notice which physical sensations you welcome, which ones you dislike.
- Notice the thoughts that come up around the physical experience of constriction, of openness.

Reflect:

- Reflect upon ways you can encourage the quality of openness when you feel stress.
- Think about ways that you perpetuate constriction unnecessarily. For example, do you get easily annoyed under certain circumstances?
- Reflect upon ways you are a more skillful communicator when you feel open rather than defensive (constricted).

Choose:

- Choose to pause and be curious about the state of constriction, rather than reacting to it.
- Choose to cultivate states which bring openness—like generosity, kindness, and compassion.

Act:

- When you feel constriction in your body, breathe deeply into it. How does the breath change the experience?
- When you have a difference of opinion with someone, approach the other person as someone to understand (openness) rather than diminish or confront (constriction).
- When you feel uncomfortable, get up and move—dance, sing, swirl around—and see if this changes your experience of discomfort.

Chapter 6 Practices: Improve the Quality of Your Thinking

Awareness:
- Bring greater awareness to the quality and content of your thoughts.
- Notice when you are having a flurry of thoughts. Notice when your thoughts are quiet.
- Bring awareness to the difference in thought as background activity in your mind and thought as direct reflection.

Reflect:
- Think about the ways the content of your thoughts influences your decisions and actions.
- Reflect on times when you "think" in a way that clutters your mind. When might you confuse overthinking for skillful reflection?
- Reflect upon the kind of biases you have that impact your ability to think flexibly and creatively.

Choose:
- Choose to engage daily in practices which quiet your mind.
- Choose to limit your attention being pulled by digital technology. For example, put the phone away when taking in information or experience (e.g., conversations, reading, walking).
- Choose to be skeptical of the usefulness of certain thoughts.

Act:
- Place yourself in environments that lend themselves to skillful reflection.
- Record the results of conscious reflection in different ways (e.g., writing, recording, sharing with others.) This helps you integrate them more.
- Participate in activities that cultivate the kind of thinking that adds to your well-being (e.g., books, film, music, seminars).

Chapter 7 Practices: Ask Questions
That Help You Think Better

Awareness:

- Become aware of how often your mind tries to make sense of things by *thinking about* rather than direct reflection.
- Notice your experience of asking yourself direct questions and regarding your answers with openness. How does this differ from *thinking about* what happened?
- Notice what you pay attention to when asking yourself the question, "What's happening now?" Do you tend to notice things within you? external events?

Reflect:

- Ask yourself "What is happening now?" throughout your day, every day.
- When you notice yourself playing something over and over in your head, ask yourself, out loud, "What is my question?" and "Do I have a question?"
- And ask yourself another question, out loud, "What, if anything, can I do to help me deepen my understanding?"

Choose:

- Choose to practice direct reflection by using simple helpful questions like, "What is happening now?", "How is this for me?", and "Is this true for me?"
- Choose to ask yourself questions in a state of openness and curiosity.
- Choose to approach the questions you ask with sincerity. Ask in a way that invites skillful reflection, and listen to your responses.

Act:

- Pay attention when your answers to your inquiries compel you to take action.
- When you take action, bring skillful reflection to the outcome of your action. What can be learned is often more important than the outcome.

Chapter 8 Practices: Take More Interest
in What Can Be Known

Awareness:
- Be aware of when you are making causal links that are not based on what you know.
- Notice how difficult it is to let go of the stories about what can't be known when you are uncomfortable or upset.
- Notice whether you make causal links when something good happens. Is this different from when something happens that you don't like?

Reflect:
- Reflect on how much time you spend lost in thought about what cannot be known.
- Think about how, in times of uncertainty, you can practice reflecting only upon what you can know, rather than conjecture.
- Reflect on ways to skillfully explore what can be known.

Choose:
- Choose to take responsibility over what you have control over, which is your response to external events.
- Choose to not personalize outcomes that you can't control.
- Choose to shift your thoughts from what cannot be known to what can be known.

Act:
- As above, ask yourself, out loud, "What can be known right now?"
- When something makes you uncomfortable, write down on a piece of paper what is happening within you. Write down what is most painful or uncomfortable. Write down what, if anything, you could do to release the discomfort.
- When something is going how you would like it to go, write down on a piece of paper what, if anything, you can know about what you have done to bring it about.

Chapter 9 Practices: How to Make Deliberate Decisions

Awareness:
- Bring awareness to the number and variety of decisions you make in a typical day.
- Bring awareness to decisions that are most urgent or relevant to your core values.

Reflect:
- Reflect on decisions that take time and thought but do not add to your life. How might you reduce time spent on these decisions?
- Reflect on which decisions are easier for you to make. Which ones are harder?
- Reflect upon areas where you are a skillful decision-maker, as well as upon areas where you might practice becoming more skillful.

Choose:
- Choose an area where it is difficult to make a decision and explore what, if anything, could help you feel better able to choose.
- Prioritize carving time out for reflection on decisions that are related to important goals.
- Choose to routinize decisions that take time and don't add to your life (e.g., have healthy meals at the ready; simplify your wardrobe).

Act:
- Spend less time in distracting activities (e.g., internet surfing) that interfere with your more actively choosing how to best engage with your free time.
- Read a book on decision-making bias (e.g., *Predictably Irrational* by Dan Ariely or *The Invisible Gorilla: How Our Intuitions Deceive Us* by Christopher Chabris and Daniel Simons).
- When making important decisions, ask for input from informed people with different perspectives.

Chapter 10 Practices: How to Choose Now and Stay Open to Unknowns

Awareness:
- Notice what you do with options that don't seem readily available. Do you move on? Do you explore them further?
- Notice when you feel fear around making a decision. Notice how fear impacts your ability to choose well.

Reflect:
- Think about a decision that is complex. Create options around this decision that you have not yet thought of. Reflect on them as if they were a real possibility.
- Think about a decision you made in which the end result was something you had not foreseen, both positive and negative. Reflect on how the outcome impacted your future decision-making.
- Think about a decision you would make if you didn't fear a negative outcome.

Choose:
- If you choose not to pursue a goal, make it conscious. Choose to choose. Consciously let go of an option rather than avoid making a decision about it.
- Choose to test out possibilities that extend beyond your current experience.
- When making decisions, choose options that reflect a belief that good things can happen for you. Then consider what conditions you can try to create to manifest these things.

Act:
- Take one small step toward a long-range goal. Then evaluate the impact of that step.
- If you feel resistance to making a difficult decision, write down different possible choices. Write down what gets in the way of you making a decision. Write down what could help you decide (e.g., information? courage? time?).
- Talk to one or two people you trust about a decision that you want to make but are unclear how to move forward.

Chapter 11 Practices: How to Be an Effective Actor

Awareness:
- Bring greater awareness to the way you approach and take action.
- Notice the difference in your experience of intentional inaction and avoiding taking action.
- Notice the experience in your body when you feel reactive. Watch the sense of urgency. Notice if it passes. Notice what keeps it alive.

Reflect:
- Think about your style of acting in different areas of our life. Think of times your style has served your aspirations and when it hasn't.
- Think about your core values and how you can bring them more front and center through meaningful action.
- Reflect upon action that can be automated as well as actions which would benefit from greater intention.

Choose:
- Choose to be more conscious of when action, and inaction, is the best option.
- Choose to create time for non-doing, for activities that have no stated goal, ones that create a sense of openness and in which you are relaxed and have a heightened awareness of what is around you.
- Choose to spend less time in actions that are neither intentional action or mindful inaction. Choose to spend less time in distracting defaults.

Act:
- Think of something that you want to have happen in your life but have not yet taken action. In the coming week, take one small action in that direction.
- When your core values require action, take it.
- When you find yourself jumping into action before pausing, refrain from action and allow more room for the experience of receptivity.

Chapter 12 Practices: How to Value
Effort Over Outcome

Awareness:
- When taking action, place your attention on the quality of your effort.
- Notice if you have expectations for a particular outcome. If you do, can you create some distance from it? Expectations limit flexibility of your future actions.
- When you are disappointed in an outcome, notice your experience as a result. What are your feelings? Thoughts?

Reflect:
- When taking action toward a goal, reflect on what you have control over and what you do not.
- Reflect upon your definition of success. In what areas might your definitions of success be narrow and limit you?
- Think about how you can stay committed to your aspirations while remaining flexible in how you get there.

Choose:
- Choose to be more interested in the quality of the effort that you bring to an action.
- Choose to be less interested in winning.
- Choose to view disappointing outcomes as an inevitable part of taking meaningful action. How might doing so change your approach to future action?

Act:
- Practice taking intentional action on what is here right now.
- When you are waiting for something to happen, take intentional action in some other area of your life. This will help you shift out of a state-of-waiting.
- Practice moving on from disappointment by learning from experience and continuing to take meaningful action.

Chapter 13 Practices: How to Work Skillfully with Stuck-ness

Awareness:
- Notice how you experience feeling stuck. What are the physical sensations?
- Notice the difference in your energy when you feel stuck and when you feel free to act.
- When you take a small action toward a goal, notice the change in energy. Does it give you a lift in energy?

Reflect:
- Reflect upon when you have felt stuck in the past few months. Where were you? What action were you trying to take?
- Reflect upon a time when you avoided what you intended to do. What were you avoiding?
- Think about some action that you would want to take right now if you felt as if nothing prevented you from taking it.

Choose:
- When you are having difficulty taking action, choose to consciously step away and take action in an area where there is no resistance. Then return and see if the experience of resistance has changed. Repeat as needed.
- Choose to engage, don't wait to be inspired!
- When you feel inspired, choose to step up and take meaningful action. Strike while the iron is hot.

Act:
- Take one small step toward a goal. Evaluate. Take another step.
- Don't take action that distracts you from meaningful action.
- If you feel stuck, be physically active and step outside your typical routine.

Chapter 14 Practices: The Benefits of Joining With Your Experience

Awareness:
- Notice the quality of your experience when you allow it to unfold.
- Notice when you feel impatient with experience and interrupt it.
- Notice when you are having an effortless experience; things are coming to you without your having to try.

Reflect:
- Think about how you allow experience to unfold more organically when you feel open and relaxed.
- Reflect on something that is hard to let go of. It might be material things, feelings, a relationship or beliefs of how things ought to be.
- Now think about ways you might loosen your grip on the things that you listed above.

Choose:
- Choose to carve out time for yourself that is not goal-directed, engaging in activities just for the sake of it.
- Choose to keep your awareness on the present moment. Choose to bring it back when your mind moves off the present moment.
- Choose to create more space for the other people in conversations, actively listening without quickly responding or filtering what is said through existing viewpoints.

Act:
- Engage in activities where you do not have specific places to be or anything to accomplish. These kinds of activities are important as a creative backdrop for realizing your aspirations.
- Try to relate to all your actions with increased focus. Multitask less.
- Practice the act of letting go. Donate things you don't use. Approach relationships with openness to change. Challenge your beliefs that limit you.

SELECTED BIBLIOGRAPHY

Alter, Adam. *Irresistible: The Rise of Addictive Technology and the Business of Keeping Us Hooked.* New York: Penguin Press, 2017.

Ariely, Dan. *Predictably Irrational, Revised and Expanded Edition: The Hidden Forces That Shape Our Decisions.* New York: Harper Perennial, 2010.

Bachhel, Rachna, and Thaman, Richa Ghay. "Effective Use of Pause Procedure to Enhance Student Engagement and Learning." *Journal of Clinical and Diagnostic Research,* 8, no. 8 (2014): 1-3.

Batchelor, Stephen. *Buddhism Without Beliefs: A Contemporary Guide to Awakening.* New York: Riverhead Books, 1998.

Bohm, David. *The Essential David Bohm,* Edited by Lee Nichols. New York: Routledge, 2002.

Boorstein, Sylvia. *Happiness is an Inside Job.* New York: Ballantine, 2007.
Brach, Tara. *Radical Acceptance: Embracing Your Life with the Heart of the Buddha.* New York: Bantam, 2003.

Chabris, Christopher, and Simons, Daniel. *The Invisible Gorilla: How Our Intuitions Deceive Us.* New York: Harmony, 2011.

Chodron, Pema. *Taking the Leap: Freeing Ourselves from Old Habits and Fears.* (Reprint) Boulder: Shambhala Publications, 2010.

Chodron, Pema. *When Things Fall Apart: Heart Advice for Difficult Times.* Boulder: Shambhala Publications, 2000.

Claxton, Guy. *Intelligence in the Flesh: Why Your Mind Needs Your Body Much More Than It Thinks.* New Haven: Yale University Press, 2016.
Damasio, Antonio. *The Feeling of What Happens: Body and Emotion in the*

Making of Consciousness. Boston: Mariner Books, 2000.

de Botton, Alain. *The Consolations of Philosophy.* New York: Vintage, 2000.

Goldstein, Joseph. *Mindfulness: A Practical Guide to Awakening.* Sounds True, 2013.

Goleman, Daniel, and Davidson, Richard. *Altered Traits: Science Reveals How Meditation Changes Your Mind, Brain, and Body.* New York: Avery, 2017.

Grafton, Ben, and MacLeod, Colin. "A Positive Perspective on Attentional Bias: Affectivity and Attentional Bias to Positive Information." *Journal of Happiness Studies*, 18, no. 4 (2017): 1029-1043.

Hartley, Catherine A. and Phelps, Elizabeth A. "Anxiety and Decision-Making." *Biological Psychiatry*, 72, no. 2 (2012): 113-118.

James, William. *Pragmatism and Other Writings.* Edited by Giles Gunn. New York: Penguin, 2000.

Kahneman, Daniel. *Thinking, Fast and Slow.* New York: Farrar, Straus, and Giroux, 2011.

Kegan, Robert, Laskow Lahey, Lisa, Miller, Matthew, and Fleming, Andy. *An Everyone Culture: Becoming a Deliberately Developmental Organization.* Boston: Harvard Business Review Press, 2016.

Killingsworth, Matthew A., and Gilbert, Daniel T. "A Wandering Mind is An Unhappy Mind." *Science*, 330, no. 6006 (2010): 932.

Kornfeld, Jack. *The Wise Heart: A Guide to the Universal Teachings of Buddhist Psychology.* New York: Bantam, 2009.

LeDoux, Joseph E., & Pine, Daniel S.(2016). "Using Neuroscience to Help Understand Fear and Anxiety: A Two-System Framework." *The American Journal of Psychiatry*, 173, no. 11(2016): 1083-1093.

Lents, Nathan H. *Not So Different: Finding Human Nature in Animals.* New York: Columbia University Press, 2016.

Merton, Thomas. *Contemplative Prayer.* New York: Doubleday (Image Classics), 1971. First published 1969.

Nouwen, Henri J.M. *The Way of the Heart: Connecting With God Through Prayer, Wisdom, and Silence.* New York: Ballantine Books, 2003.

Redish, David A. *The Mind Within the Brain: How We Make Decisions and How Those Decisions Go Wrong.* New York: Oxford University Press, 2013.

Salzberg, Sharon. *Real Happiness.* New York: Workman, 2010.

Schwartz, Jeffrey M., and Gladding, Rebecca. *You Are Not Your Brain: The 4-Step Solution for Changing Habits, Ending Unhealthy Thinking, and Taking Control of Your Life.* New York: Avery, 2011.

Seligman, Martin E.P. *Flourish: A Visionary New Understanding of Happiness and Well-Being.* New York: Atria Books, 2012.

Siegel, Daniel J. *The Developing Mind.* New York: Guilford Press, 2012.

Suzuki, Shunryu. *Zen Mind, Beginner's Mind.* Boston: Shambhala Publications, 2006. First published 1973.
Thich Nhat Hanh. *The Miracle of Mindfulness: An Introduction to the Practice of Meditation.* Boston: Beacon Press, 1999. First published 1975.

van der Kolk, Bessel. *The Body Keeps the Score: Brain, Mind, and Body in Healing Trauma.* New York: Penguin Books, 2015.

Vroling, Maartje S., Glashouwer, Klaske A., Lange, Wolf-Gero, Allart-van Dam, E., and de Jong, Peter J. "What I believe is true: Belief-confirming reasoning bias in social anxiety disorder." *Journal of Behavior Therapy and Experimental Psychiatry*, 53 (2016): 9-16.

Watts, Alan. *Does It Matter?: Essays on Man's Relation to Materiality*. New York: Vintage, 1971. First published in 1958.

Watts, Alan. *Become What You Are*. Expanded edition. Boulder: Shambhala Publications, 2003. First published in 1955.

About the author

PHOTO: TODD ESTRIN

A psychologist with nearly three decades of clinical and consulting experience, Lisa Kentgen, Ph.D. has taught intentional practices everywhere from the psychotherapy office to companies to the classroom. She has served on faculty at Columbia University Teachers College and as a clinical director within a research center for childhood mood and anxiety disorders at New York State Psychiatric Institute. Dr. Kentgen has published scientific articles on topics including the development of conscious awareness, the biological correlates of depression and anxiety, and identifying emotional difficulties in children. Dr. Kentgen believes passionately in the need for greater authenticity in the world today, and that transformation happens when one person at a time commits to living with intention. She lives in Brooklyn, New York.

www.drlisakentgen.com